SOMETHING IS MISSING

MITCH FROST

WESTBOW
PRESS®
A DIVISION OF THOMAS NELSON
& ZONDERVAN

Copyright © 2023 Mitch Frost.

All rights reserved. No part of this book may be used or reproduced by any means, graphic, electronic, or mechanical, including photocopying, recording, taping or by any information storage retrieval system without the written permission of the author except in the case of brief quotations embodied in critical articles and reviews.

This book is a work of non-fiction. Unless otherwise noted, the author and the publisher make no explicit guarantees as to the accuracy of the information contained in this book and in some cases, names of people and places have been altered to protect their privacy.

WestBow Press books may be ordered through booksellers or by contacting:

WestBow Press
A Division of Thomas Nelson & Zondervan
1663 Liberty Drive
Bloomington, IN 47403
www.westbowpress.com
844-714-3454

Because of the dynamic nature of the Internet, any web addresses or links contained in this book may have changed since publication and may no longer be valid. The views expressed in this work are solely those of the author and do not necessarily reflect the views of the publisher, and the publisher hereby disclaims any responsibility for them.

Any people depicted in stock imagery provided by Getty Images are models, and such images are being used for illustrative purposes only. Certain stock imagery © Getty Images.

Interior Image Credit: Ellen Cramplet

Scriptures marked as NLT are taken from the Holy Bible, New Living Translation, copyright © 1996, 2004, 2015 by Tyndale House Foundation. Used by permission of Tyndale House Publishers Inc., Carol Stream, Illinois 60188. All rights reserved.

Scripture marked NIV are taken from the Holy Bible, New International Version®. NIV®. Copyright © 1973, 1978, 1984 by International Bible Society. Used by permission of Zondervan. All rights reserved.

ISBN: 978-1-6642-9204-8 (sc)
ISBN: 978-1-6642-9205-5 (e)

Library of Congress Control Number: 2023902420

Print information available on the last page.

WestBow Press rev. date: 04/17/2023

Something is Missing is another great journey between ourselves and God written by Pastor Mitch Frost. Pastor Mitch blends beautifully the problems we face today with an answer that is timelessness. Sit back and enjoy the teachings that will help lead you to find what's missing in your life.

- Jeff Hedley
Columbus, Ohio

Whenever I take a trip or go to an unfamiliar place it is so nice to have some help. In Something is Missing Pastor Mitch is that someone here to help. The journey into the heart of Jesus is simple, but not easy. Having a friend walk with you as you open your mind to what may be missing in your life will ease your fears and strengthen your heart. So, get comfortable, courageous, and connect with your friend Mitch as you seek to find what is missing.

- Anthony Rex, Executive Director of BE1MK1
Columbus, Ohio

Something Is Missing is a poignant look at sin, struggle, surrender, and redemption. Frost masterfully builds mystery and suspense that will captivate readers as they go along on a journey that leads to the Cross. Prepare to be challenged and convicted, yet filled with hope and a fresh perspective of God's mercy and love. There is an exciting paradigm shift awaiting for both followers of Christ and unbelievers alike as readers discover keys to unlock treasures that will equip them to answer life's biggest questions.

- Tim Billingsley
Columbus, Ohio

In Something Is Missing my friend Mitch Frost challenges us to view our walk with God through the full scope of who God is and to confront our misconceptions about His character. Mitch's unique way of drawing you in with a simple proposition and leading you into something so much deeper makes every chapter so special. Don't skip this.

- Cody Woodlee, Lead Pastor of New Purpose Church
Murfreesboro, Tennessee

In Something Is Missing I believe you will find a real journey to THE truth. In a generation that's searching for "their truth," there is something to be said about the real WAY, TRUTH, & LIFE. I believe Mitch and his thoughts will deepen that conversation in whomever the reader may be and enrich them unto pure action. Mitch's books are deeply reflective of scripture, introspective on the soul, and encouraging to the heart. I think he tackles the question well of that something missing in the depths of a generation searching for more. I trust your perspective will be highly blessed through the process of reading this book. As you ask the question "what's missing" I pray you will find the divine solution of who Jesus is in every page.

- Mason West, Campus Pastor of Bluefield University
Bluefield, Virginia

In life we all go through times when we feel like something is missing, there is a void that needs to be filled with something. But what is that something? Is it a job, a car, money, a relationship, children – what is your something that is missing? In this book, Something Is Missing, Mitch Frost helps us all discover what could be missing in our lives. He takes us on a journey through the life of Jesus to help us all discover what is missing. Hold on tight, your world is about to be rocked. No matter what stage of life you are in, I promise you will not be the same after reading this book.

- Aundrea Hasty
Blythewood, South Carolina

For the last several years, Mitch Frost has been a friend of mine as we lead in churches near Columbus, Ohio. In his new book, Something Is Missing, Mitch invites readers on a journey to find and fully understand what it means to follow Jesus. Using personal experience, Scripture and practical application, Something Is Missing will help you discover a new perspective on what it really means to walk with the Jesus of the Bible. When you're done reading this book, pass it along to a friend. I'm certain they need it as much as you did!

- Aaron Taylor, Teaching Pastor of Living Hope Church
Columbus, Ohio

In this book, Mitch shows us beautifully that something indeed is missing through a unique look at the criminal on the cross. Sometimes we think something missing is a bad thing, when in reality we can't see the full picture of what God is doing. This book will help spur you on in your faith and challenge you to be bold for Jesus and know that He has given you exactly what you need!

- Marc Hall, Associate Pastor of Students and
Discipleship at Main Street Baptist Church
Alexandria, Kentucky

If you're in a cycle of depression, anxiety, heaviness of life or even a lack of purpose and worth, there is more for you. This book prompts such an important question "what is it that's missing?" This generation is desperate for this "something" that always seems out of reach. The moment we stop reaching for it and take a hold of what God has set before us, life starts to make sense. This book takes you through how the Lord sees you and how He desires us to see Him.

- Todd Sullivan
Columbus, Ohio

Something Is Missing is not just a book. It is a journey for everyone that will leave you wanting more after each chapter. Move past the basic Sunday school answers and let this book challenge your personal beliefs as Mitch Frost talks about the mysteries behind having a relationship with God.

- Daniel Wilt
Jackson, Michigan

In Something Is Missing, Mitch Frost has invited people to deepen their faith through a discovery. No matter where they are on their faith journey, Frost guides his readers down a path that leads to Jesus. As someone who has partnered with Mitch in ministry before, I am confident that this book will be a blessing to many.

- Micah McCoy
Columbus, Ohio

I think there becomes a pivotal moment in every Christian's faith walk where they pause. They ponder. And they have some deep moments of realization on so many different topics. I think we all have a moment, or if we're being honest, multiple moments where we think, is this really it? Surely, I'm missing something. But what is missing? We feel like we're doing all the things, we're saying all the sayings, praying all the prayers, watching, and listening and diving into our faith walk just desperate for the answer. Doing all we can in our own strength and lack thereof to figure out the answer to this void we feel sometimes. We know we were created for more; I think Mitch challenges us to delve into the nature of our humanity and what we are so blinded to being our "natural way of things" and challenges us to take a big step back and examine the things we're so comfortable seeing as normal. Making us process experiences, thoughts, and actions to help us explore and eventually come to realize what is missing. This book kept me wanting to read more, kept me optimistic in searching my own experiences and feelings and coming to terms with what's missing.

- Haley Williams
Vinta, Oklahoma

*For Charlotte,
This book was finished in a season of
expecting you. And it's being released
in a season of bringing you into our lives.
I cannot wait for the day that you find what is
missing. And you allow it to remain missing.*

CONTENTS

ACKNOWLEDGEMENTS..XIII

PART #1: THE PROBLEM

CHAPTER 1 FINDING WHAT IS MEANT TO BE MISSING 1
CHAPTER 2 THE ENDLESS PURSUIT OF MEASURING UP 13
CHAPTER 3 IF PERFECTION IS THE STANDARD 27
CHAPTER 4 THE MURDERER IN EACH OF US 41

PART #2: THE PATH

CHAPTER 5 AN UNFAIR STORY OF THE COMPLETELY FAIR GOD 55
CHAPTER 6 YOU'RE NOT THAT POWERFUL 68
CHAPTER 7 THE SCALE IS BROKEN 80
CHAPTER 8 THE MISSING PIECE THAT SOMEHOW MAKES US WHOLE 95

PART #3: THE PROPOSITION

CHAPTER 9 YOUR PICTURE ISN'T COMPLETE, BUT HIS IS 115

CHAPTER 10	LIVING FROM ACCEPTANCE, NOT FOR IT	130
CHAPTER 11	THE NEVER-ENDING DISCOVERY	144
X MARKS THE SPOT		159
ABOUT THE AUTHOR		163

ACKNOWLEDGEMENTS

There is so much that goes into bringing a book like this to life. This is the most meaningful project I've given myself to thus far in my time on earth and I want to quickly thank everyone in my corner.

First of all, Lex, my amazing wife. You allow for my passions and dreams to come to fruition and there is no one else I'd rather do life with. Thank you for always supporting me, pushing me, believing in me, and doing it all by my side. I wouldn't be able to write something like this without you behind me. You allow me to have confidence and boldness in what God asks me to do. I love you so much.

Jeff Hedley. Where do I even start with you? Sometimes God places people in our lives to allow dreams to come to life. That's exactly what you are for me. Anyone can sit on the sidelines and support, but you got your hands dirty and backed every step of this process. You're the feet to my dreams. Without you I don't think this book would be what it is. Thank you for being one of the most generous people that I know. We crossed paths for a reason and this book is proof of that. Thank you so much.

Anthony Rex, I was stuck before we sat down and had the conversation that moved this entire thing forward. You and your family are incredible gifts to me, and my family and you have an incredible gift for coaching and moving people like me towards their goals and dreams. Without you, launching this book wouldn't have happened the way that it did. Thank you for cheering me on, sharpening me when needed, and seeing my goals as possible.

Tucker Johnson, thank you for the work you put in to design this book and capture the essence of me in it. Thank you for working with me and being willing to take shots and think outside of the box for what this book could look like. As soon as this thing started to take shape, I knew I wanted you behind it. You are so undeniably talented, and you prove it time and time again. Thank you for sharing some of your talents with this project.

To all of my friends and family who read this book, called me out where I was wrong in it, wrote openings for it, helped spread the word for it, launched it, and cheered it on, thank you. These past two years of having the idea and bringing it out wouldn't of happened without you all. I'm incredibly thankful for each and every one of you.

You've all shaped this book, and me as a person, in your own way. And I'll never be able to thank you enough.

What Is This Thing?

Something is missing. Seriously. The math doesn't add up. The formula falls short. Something is off. Are you getting this? The scale is uneven. The balance is broken. Something isn't right. And nothing that we could ever do would be able to course-correct this imbalance. Nothing in our ability or power can balance the scale or patch the hole.

Isn't it frustrating?

Can you feel it—that sense that something is missing from your life? How would you describe this realization? Is it good? Is it bad? Is it a little bit scary? Does this lack of the thing cause you to wonder how to get it back and where it may be hiding? Are you better off without this thing?

We have to get to the bottom of this.

If you're like me, you like things that add up, make sense, and have solutions. This whatever-it-is that's not right simply won't do. If you're forced to reconcile with something that's missing and that you can't find on your own, shouldn't you just give up?

Will we ever be complete if something is missing?

The horribly beautiful answer to that question is no and yet yes. Something will always be missing, and because of what's missing, we can rest in being made complete. Does this sound like a paradox? A miscalculation? A misuse of information or a bad retelling of a story?

I agree with you.

That's why this book is here. The reason why this book is in your hands right now is because I became obsessed with what was missing. I became hooked on the idea that something was and is missing in our story, and not only that—but we should be thankful because of it. Now, if you're reading this and expecting me to give you the answer right off the bat—I'm sorry, but it's just not going to be that easy. Instead, I'm going to offer a journey. A process. A walk through the story of humanity's brokenness pinned up against the undeniable perfection of the God of the Bible. And what will you find, you may ask.

That something is missing.

And this missing something is very important. It's borderline crucial to the way you live and the things you do. And by borderline, I mean absolutely, for sure. In fact, when you find what is missing, and not only that but learn to accept what is missing, your entire understanding of who God is and what He's done for you may completely change. It may ignite a fire and desire to follow God in a way that you've never had or known before. It may allow you to escape the pitfalls of comparison, achievement, and competition. But we are going to have to find it first.

Are you ready to dig deep and search?

I want to invite you into this discovery journey with me. I want to walk alongside you in these pages and experience everything that the Father has for us. And I know what you may be thinking: *Are you really going to have us read this book, just to come to the conclusion that God is the thing that's missing?*

No. Even if you're reading this right now, and you would say that God isn't a part of your life or you don't believe in Him, I do believe He is missing in your life. Why do I hold that stance? Because I believe that He is the Creator of the entire universe, and He loves you and cares for you regardless of what you've done—which is a huge deal.

But if you're reading this book right now as someone who believes in God and has a relationship with Jesus, don't be afraid. I'm not going to lead you to a simple solution that you've known all along. The thing that's missing is something that will impact and shape how you relate to God in so many ways, and I'm pretty confident that even if you've lived your whole life believing in Him, this thing will still impact you greatly.

What I'm trying to say is this: if you're someone who doesn't believe in God, this book will speak to you. As we walk through this journey and discover what's missing, you are also going to find the heart of Christianity, Jesus. You're also going to find some things that may contradict what you've heard in the past about those who call themselves Christians (those people who heap piles of guilt and shame onto your life).

If you're someone who does believe in God, whether that be for just the last couple days or for as long as you can remember, the thing that you're going to find in this book will challenge what you believe and allow you to step into an understanding, appreciation, and relationship with God that's more beautiful than you could've imagined.

So, whoever you are, and wherever you are—are you ready to find this thing? This missing, unachievable, irrevocable thing?

Now, even though I don't want to reveal what this missing thing is just yet, I do want to be upfront with you about how we're going to attempt to discover it. Consider this our battle plan, our treasure map, or our GPS for getting to, unlocking, and opening up this missing thing.

This book is going to move in three parts. Three distinct sections will move us through the story of us, God, and this missing thing in a smooth and understandable way. By dividing this work into three sections, it'll allow us to walk away with real, applicable, raw truths in order to change the way we live and interact with God. Our three parts are "The Problem," "The Path," and "The Proposition."

Let's start with "The Problem." For the first couple chapters of this journey together, we're going to take a deep look at what's wrong. At what isn't working. Whether it be in American Christianity as a whole or in our own personal approaches and responses to God, we need to uncover what's broken inside of us (don't worry, this isn't a depressing book; it's actually very much the opposite). If we use this as our starting place, it's going to show us the universal problem pressing on all of us, which will create the space in our minds to find a solution. In each chapter in "The Problem" section, you're going to be given clues to find what is missing.

After we've figured out what isn't working in our lives, we're going to shift gears and move on to "The Path." In this meaty section, I want to walk through the story of the God of the Bible and why He had to do the things that He's done (like allowing His only Son to be murdered). This is where we'll discover what's really missing. And believe me when I say that it's not going to be what you think. There's something beautiful about digging deep and discovering an aspect of God that you may not have heard before. And that's exactly what this section is going to do. Once you get to this place in the book, the secret of what's left out is going to start to be uncovered, but this doesn't explicitly mean it'll be unlocked. So for this section, each chapter will leave you with a key that can be used to unlock what's missing.

But there's one more extremely important section left: "The Proposition." After we've spent so much time and effort discovering and uncovering what isn't working, what's truly lost from this picture, and who God is, I don't want to leave a single reader hanging. That is why this book will end with a proposition, an offer to change the way that we view and treat God in our own lives in order to see radical life change. This section will present the choice to accept what's missing and live from it instead of without it. To conclude our journey together, each chapter will end with a treasure or a takeaway that can radically change your life and perspective on your walk with God.

Along with these three parts, I am going to do my best to help translate these ideas in the most simple and impactful way possible. In order to do that, I want to strive to include personal stories, quotes, and Scripture that will allow us not only to digest what is being said but also to stand firm on the fact that it comes from the Word of God, which holds all truth.

Not only this, but I'm going to ask you to time-travel once again (if you've read my first book, *Love More, Worry Less*, you know exactly where I'm going with this point). I'm going to paint an imaginary story in each chapter where I will ask you, the reader, to travel back in time to 33 AD and enter into a story taking place in Jerusalem. How you choose to fill in the gaps of this imaginary tale in your own mind is up to you, but I will provide the characters, plot, and dialogue. The reason why I enjoy including these types of stories in these books is because it allows us to imagine a historical moment through the lens of a background character. It allows us to feel the weight of what was going on in Bible times, which helps us better understand the things we read in God's Word. And can I just say that I'm extremely excited about the imaginary journey that you'll find on these pages? I hope you enjoy it, too.

Are we ready to get started? I've provided you with the process and steps that we're going to take on this journey together. I've done my best to hide and disguise what has disappeared because, believe me, it's going to be worth finding on your own.

So here we go. Buckle up. It's go-time.

Let's begin the pursuit of what is missing.

PART #1

THE PROBLEM

Chapter 1

FINDING WHAT IS MEANT TO BE MISSING

Today's the day, I thought to my ten-year-old self as I stared at the gigantic roller coaster that stood in front of me.

Pretty much every year for as long as I can remember, my family got season passes to Kings Island, which is an amusement park about an hour and a half from where I grew up. We'd spend a lot of our summer days driving up to the park, getting there before it got busy, riding rides all afternoon, and then leaving whenever it got too hot or once the lines were too long. Pretty awesome, isn't it?

I loved roller coasters at the time. Okay let me rephrase that: I *wanted* to love roller coasters at the time. Whenever we'd go, I'd find myself in an internal battle as I'd walk up to the big coasters, even get in line sometimes, just to walk away or chicken out before I actually got on. This happened every single time for years. But as I stood in line on this particular day, I told myself that it was going to be different, that I'd finally conquer my fear.

This particular ride had just opened that summer, and it was called "The Diamondback." 215-foot drop. Eighty miles an hour. Downright terrifying, if we're being honest. But I decided that day, I was going to do it. And if I could just ride this giant ride (which at the time was the tallest one in their park), then nothing could stand in my way.

As we drew closer and closer to the carts, my nervous energy grew more and more unbearable. I could hear the screams as the riders went down the hill in front of me, and I could see the workers casually sending people to their deaths. It seemed psychotic. I could feel the sweat collecting in my armpits.

"I don't think I'm going to do it today. I'm too scared," I said as we got ready to get on after over an hour of waiting in line. There was a small group of us in line together, including a few of my siblings and my mom. As soon as that statement of being too afraid left my mouth, I felt my mom look at me for a moment, and then she leaned over and said, "You're always going to feel a little bit of fear when you ride rides like these. That's the point! If you lose the excitement that the fear causes, then why would anyone ride them?"

Now, hold on a minute. Was she telling me that some things are missing for a reason? Better yet, was she telling me that sometimes a lack of something (in this case courage) would actually end up benefiting me? Now that is a concept we can work with.

I rode "The Diamondback" that day. And it was terrifying. But from that day forward, I rode every ride that I came up against. And it wasn't because I suddenly had enough inner strength and courage to make myself not afraid of them. Rather, it was because I accepted what was supposed to be missing, and I embraced the natural fear, excitement, and joy that roller coasters are supposed to bring.

As we really begin this search for what is missing, I have a feeling that I'm obligated to share some bad news. And if you're a reader who's fully committed to this idea of a search for this missing something, then consider this your first clue:

The fact that something is missing may be for our good.

Just like the fear of roller coasters that actually ends up working in our favor because it preserves the ultimate feelings of fear and excitement, what we're going to find in this book may actually preserve something for us as well. It's going to preserve our lives as we follow and glorify God to the best of our ability. Dare I say, it will protect us from burn out, a lackadaisical faith, and so much more.

But before we get there, we need to identify the problem in each of us. The problem that is running rampant and spitting in the face of what Jesus has done for us. Its name? Striving.

Our problem is that we're tryhards. I know this section is titled "The Problem," and we're going to continue to get more and more into what this universal problem is, but for a lot of us, it starts right here in the conversation of striving. Deep down in our cores, this is something that many of us struggle with to some degree or in some arena of life. Without even realizing it, we are trying as hard as we possibly can to earn our way into God's grace, love, and acceptance (or somebody else's). For some of us, this is because of a lack of acceptance we felt from our parents growing up or in relationships that we've had. For some of us, this is because the battles of depression and anxiety own our minds. For some of us, this is because of unbearable trauma that we've experienced at some point in our lives. And for some of us, this is simply because we've bought into the lie that modern-day American Christianity (and culture in general) is selling, that we must live up to an imaginary standard of "good enough."

You don't think this applies to you? Let me ask you a question, then. When was the last time you made a commitment to God and then didn't follow through with it? If you're like me, this happens way too often. Maybe you made the commitment to read your Bible more often, to give more money to your church or those in need, to stop gossiping about people in your life. I don't know what it is for you, but think about a promise that you've made God. Maybe it lasted a day. Maybe a month. Maybe a couple years. But I'm going to assume that, at some point, you failed and let God down.

If you can think of a time like that, what was your reaction? What did your thoughts, heart, and mind tell you when you fell short? That God was going to be mad at you? That God viewed you as less important in Heaven now? That somehow the failed promise on your part made His love for you less intimate or less overwhelmingly awesome?

Maybe, for some of you reading, you haven't let God down on a commitment or promise that you've made to Him because you aren't sure if you believe in Him or you say you do but following Him looks like a church service on Christmas and Easter, and that's about it. (Oh snap! I just went there.) I'd argue that you still can find yourself in these words, and you may be stuck in the same trap of trying to be good enough. At work or at home, when you let someone down or fail to do what you said you were going to do, how do you feel? What's your reaction like? Did you feel like the person's love or appreciation of you decreased when you messed up?

Every single one of us has felt this way and actively feels these ways—definitely with the people in our lives, but also with God. And the reason why we feel these ways is because we view our actions as directly correlated with God's level of love for us. This is natural! Our best gauge for love is based on the love given and received by those around us, and if we're being honest, if we broke promises and commitments to them on a weekly basis or talked to them only on Sundays, they'd probably love us less, right?

But the cold hard truth is that we can't view God the same

way. God's love doesn't work that way. Maybe we can even say that based on our human standards, God's love is a little bit unnatural! Maybe even supernatural. If you have a relationship with Jesus, He loves you today just as much as He did yesterday—yes, even with what happened last night. But more on this later.

The fact that we view God's love this way is directly connected to the fact that we think we have to earn God's love. You and I both live inside our own minds and do things, say things, and even go places in hopes that the result will be more of God's (or other's) love poured out on us.

And the hard part for us is this way of life is simply not scriptural. This faith that's based on how we measure up does not exist or hold water in terms of what the Bible says. In fact, what we find echoed throughout God's Word is the idea that our salvation isn't based on us at all. In fact, it's based on God.

Not sold on this yet? Just check out what Paul has to say on this subject in Ephesians 2. After going on an incredibly Spirit-driven rant at the beginning of this chapter, Paul says this: "God saved you by his grace when you believed. And you can't take credit for this; it is a gift from God. Salvation is not a reward for the good things we have done, so none of us can boast about it" (Ephesians 2:8-9, NLT).

Very interesting. And this is not the only time this idea is conveyed on the pages of our bibles. In fact, it's an idea that is crucial if you want to understand and get on board with what Jesus has done for us as a whole. The entire point of the bloody sacrifice on the cross was for this very purpose! So that we could enter into the gates of Heaven and into the family of God not based on our striving but based entirely on His saving. Because we simply cannot do it, no matter how good we may seem.

Now, we're really getting somewhere. We're starting to uncover the first step in this process of finding what's missing—coming to terms with our brokenness. Once we get to the part of this process where what is missing is truly revealed (and that time is coming), it is going to become much more beautiful and freeing if we have this moment of reflection in our own inner worlds first—that we are, in fact, broken people in need of fixing.

If this is your first time hearing the fact that you're a broken person and always have been, it may come off as a bit of a downer. I'm extremely sorry for that. I've said it before, and I'll say it again that this book may feel sad at first, but the payoff is going to be immensely worth it. The discovery that's waiting in these chapters is worth the initial shock of realizing that you and me and every person you've ever known is broken. Yes, even your grandma.

Coming to terms with our brokenness actually means we're coming to terms with our humanity. If we really want to better understand the story of God, then these things cannot be separated. Now don't get me wrong; you have value. You have so much worth. Your identity is rooted in the Creator of the universe, and the further we go on this journey together, the more you're going to discover of that beautiful reality. I mean, right off the bat, in the first book of the Bible, we're told that we are created in God's image, and we're supposed to rule and reign with Him (Genesis 1:27-28). Nothing else on planet earth has that description!

But you're also broken. In fact, in the Bible, which consists of sixty-six books and 1,189 chapters, humanity gets two of those chapters in one of those books, where we aren't broken. Yay us! What a track record. Those chapters where we get to shine are Genesis 1–2.

Just to catch you up to speed on what's going on here, in Genesis 1, the opening chapter of the story of God and the world, God breathes everything into existence. Literally everything. The sun, the moon, the galaxies, the birds, the trees, mankind, every single thing. This first chapter of Scripture is full of wonder and beauty as our amazingly creative God flexes His creative process, and Thanos snaps the world around us into reality. There's never been an artist like Him, and there never will be. Sorry, Bob Ross.

And just a quick side note on God that's important for our conversation is that He is the Creator. Wow! What a deep thought, am I right? But think about it. Everything else you see, touch, feel, love, and interact with is created. It came from something or someone else and was a byproduct of another thing. God is no byproduct. God is *the* product and the inventor of it all. No one created God because He's always been and will always be, and that's precisely what makes Him God. He is holy, set apart, Creator, and not created.

Anyway, back to the story of humanity.

After the world is created, God decides that humans shouldn't be alone, and so He hooks his homie Adam up with a partner, an equal companion, someone to do life with, and her name is Eve. They continue to walk with God, naming animals and living in this beautiful utopia that God has created called the Garden of Eden. Now, unlike most utopias, which are imaginary, this place was real, and it was insanely beautiful.

But then, the timer on our two chapters of stardom runs out. Our awesome time of being the good guys is over. Genesis chapter 3: in the world of Christianity, this is called "The Fall." As you may have heard, a serpent (aka Satan) comes along and convinces Adam and Eve to eat from the one tree that God has instructed them not to eat from. Cue those memes that read, "You had one job!"

Suddenly, everything shifts. In fact, the repercussions of this singular moment are seen in ways that we can't even fully comprehend: the pain of childbirth, joyless labor, jealousy, competition, disease, pain, mental illness, strongholds, and so much more.

Ladies and gentlemen, sin has entered our story. It has destroyed and corrupted the perfect world that God has designed for us.

And from this moment on, you and I and every human born into this world are born into sin. Built into our DNA and genetic makeup and psychology is this thing called sin. It's an earthly desire to do what God doesn't want us to do. And even when we follow God, there are remains of false motives, jealousy, pride, anger, gossip, and so much more.

Silly snake.

Now, because of this tragic situation, the journey of God's redemption begins. The ultimate game plan for God to save us is put into action. Because of one apple? Seems a little bit dramatic. Well, not exactly. Not when you begin to adapt the biblical perspective of who God is and how holy He has always been. Once we see God in this way, then we understand that this one sin committed by Adam and Eve is extremely serious because a perfect God cannot coexist with broken people. We have a serious problem on our hands. In fact, we may be the problem.

God's plan for the redemption of humanity can only be fulfilled if we accept that something is meant to be missing. We're one step closer to discovering what it may be.

✟

Sunrise already? you think to yourself as the bright, warm rays shine through your bedroom window and into your eyes, causing you to wake up earlier than you expected.

Sometimes you find yourself awakened by the sun in a pleasant way, almost like it's a natural alarm clock calling you out of bed and into the day that's before you.

But today—well, that's not the case. It's Saturday. The Sabbath. You deserve some more time to sleep. So you turn over, pull the blankets over your face, and return to a state of unconsciousness.

"You did *WHAT*?!"

Suddenly, you're zapped back into reality by your father yelling from the kitchen downstairs.

SOMETHING IS MISSING

What time is it? Where am I? Am I late for work? All of the confused questions rush into your mind as you sit up and rub your eyes. You aren't entirely sure if you fell back asleep for five minutes or five days.

"For the last time, you cannot continue to act like this and remain in our household. In our family for that matter. People talk. And the reputation that you're creating for this family is anything but honorable. If you stay on this path, you're going to wind up in a place that there is no coming back from," your father continues.

Oh brother, you think to yourself. Literally. This loud conversation that woke you up from your sleep has to do with your older brother. As it always does. Everything bad in your home seems to revolve around your older brother, his terrible decisions, and your parent's inability to see the light at the end of the tunnel with the way he chooses to act.

This is just another average, ordinary, and somewhat commonplace day in your household. Your parents are yelling at your brother for some horrendous new thing that he's done, and you're just trying to keep your head down and stay out of trouble. Even with how bad he is, they probably wouldn't even notice you. At least, that's what it feels like sometimes.

As you make your way downstairs, your brother is walking toward the front door, and your parents continue to yell and follow him down the hallway. Right before he gets to the door, he turns to see you standing there, and he smirks and winks. You do it back, as you always do with each other, and before you know it, he turns and exits into the warm morning sun.

Just like that, he was gone. As usual.

Your mother angrily turns back toward the kitchen, speaking under her breath, "I just can't take this anymore. I'm going to lose it with him."

Your father remains standing at the door as you sneak behind him and into the kitchen.

Yikes. This seems to be a little bit more hostile than usual. And that's saying a lot, you think to yourself as you sit down at the kitchen table.

Your parents continue talking, not even looking your way as you begin eating breakfast and listening to their back-and-forth. Ever since your brother was a teenager, these things have been going on. He constantly finds himself in trouble whether it be just little bits of mischief or bigger problems that require the attention of the local authorities. There is always something.

Sometimes, the burden that your parents carry of dealing with and caring for a son like this who causes so much turmoil and pain weighs on you too. How could it not? You care about your parents so much, and seeing them in this type of position every day is so hard to watch. Not to mention the fact that, in this day and age, a family's reputation was everything. In fact, you sometimes live your day-to-day life with the question guarding the back of your mind, "Will this honor my parents or cause them to be ashamed?" Sometimes, this can be burdensome, but it's kept you out of a lot of trouble so far in life.

They've raised you in a comfortable, loving, Jewish environment where you've been taught what to say and do in order to remain in good standing with God. Your father is a Pharisee who teaches at the local synagogue, and due to your brother's reputation, he's been in some hot water lately with those in authority above him. They constantly question his ability to lead his own household and family, which you know weighs on him immensely, not that you'd ever say anything about it.

And your mom. Your poor mom. She is the sweetest, most honest, meek woman that you've ever known. Women in the community have always been able to come to her with their problems and struggles, and she handles them with love and grace. It's truly a beautiful thing to be raised by a mother who loves people so well. But yet again, as your brother has begun to get into more and more serious trouble, the women in your town

SOMETHING IS MISSING

have begun to pull away from her more and more. All you can do is watch as your mom slowly loses the opportunities to help and guide women in the community due to your brother's reputation.

This honor-shame culture is no joke, is it?

After multiple minutes of you watching your parents go back and forth and seeing the weight that they're feeling from this situation, you finally decide to chime in, "Hello! Yes, your other child here. What did he do this time? And also good morning, happy Sabbath, good to see you both."

Suddenly, they both turn their attention toward you, still sitting at the kitchen table. The look on their faces is as if they truly just realized that you were there—or that they are almost surprised to remember they even have a second kid.

"Um—sorry we haven't spoken to you yet. Good morning. It's not important what your brother did this time. We don't want to put those kinds of thoughts in your head. Especially on the Sabbath. Just know that it was bad and that God surely has turned His back on your brother now, if it hasn't happened already," your father explains.

Aha, you think to yourself, *there it is. The moment in every situation like this where Dad brings up the fact that this mistake is edging my brother closer to God shutting Him off forever. I mean, I guess it's only fair of them to talk this way, right? God is a just, fair, and jealous God. At least, that's what I've always been taught. And with a brother who acts this way, maybe what everyone says about him is true—that God can't forgive him, that he's messed up a few too many times, that he is going to Hell. Maybe he deserves it. I don't really know.*

Instead of speaking any of these things out loud, you simply nod your head in understanding and return to your breakfast. It is still strange, though. Your parents have told you the things he's done in the past: stealing from the market, cheating to pass his tests in school, getting in fights everywhere he goes, lying to your parents about where he's been, skipping times at the synagogue.

You've heard it all. So why won't they tell you about *this* mistake?

CLUE #1 -
THE FACT THAT SOMETHING IS MISSING MAY BE FOR OUR GOOD.

Chapter 2

THE ENDLESS PURSUIT OF MEASURING UP

Stop trying so hard to measure up. There, I said it. And I'll say it again, just to make sure you hear me loud and clear. Stop trying to measure up!

Stop trying to prove yourself. It's a trap. It's a deadly trap that is only going to leave you burnt out, lifeless, and stuck in a cycle that has no end. I'll just be upfront to start this chapter off: here's your second clue in this hunt for what's missing:

If your goal is to measure up, you're going to fail every single time.

In high school, I had a really close friend named Eli. He was someone that I could always rely on to hang out with, laugh a lot, and get into just the right amount of trouble together. What I mean by that is we'd ride the line between doing things that were mischievous but that wouldn't result in serious consequences if we ever got caught. But anyway, that's not the point of telling you about Eli.

You see, Eli was well known in high school. Or maybe I should say, he was easy to pick out of a crowd based solely on what he looked like. I'd love to know where your mind is going right now, but just keep reading.

The reason for this was because he was six feet eleven inches tall. Yes, you read that right. Almost seven feet. This kid wore size-sixteen shoes and could dunk a basketball on a ten-foot rim as a seventh grader.

He was a basketball player. (Did he have an option with stature like that? Probably not.) And he was good—like, really good. And since we hung out so often, we'd often end up playing basketball at our houses with some other friends from time to time.

But here's the deal. I'm not short, and this dude made me feel really really tiny. I'm six feet nothing, and it's not often that I'm put in the "short" category when matched up against other people my age. But walking next to him never got old because it was always a reminder of how small I really was. And when we'd play basketball together, it was as if he didn't even have to try when it came to blocking me, dunking on me, and things of that nature. Every single time I'd try to measure up to him or challenge his size, I'd get beat. So, in order to even begin to have fun while playing these driveway basketball games, I had to switch my strategy and try something new.

I stopped trying to measure up—plain and simple. I stopped allowing our heights to be the determining factor of how the game would go because, time and time again, I'd get destroyed in the games we'd play. Basketball was never my strongest sport, but I've always been athletic, so I adapted my game to focus more on speed, shooting, and getting away from Eli while on the court. And the results? Well, he still beat me every time, dunked over top of me, and often broke my ankles with his ball handles, but that's beside the point!

My point is, it's time for us to break the endless cycle and pursuit of trying to measure up in our walk with God. The pill that we have to swallow (and to some of us, it will feel like a very, very big pill) is that if we try to measure up to others when it comes to our faith, the results are going to be detrimental, and they're going to stop us in our tracks from ever getting close to what God has planned for us. In fact, maybe the smartest thing we can do is accept how small we really are.

The psalmist puts it beautifully here, "What is mankind that you are mindful of them, human beings that you care for them?" (Psalm 8:4, NIV). We are small compared to the holy, perfect God of the Bible! Let this sink in.

This danger of measuring up may make you feel that you're discovering what's missing for a season, but I promise you it won't last. Let's play this out in a couple different ways.

Let's start with the danger of trying to measure up to those around you. Maybe a better way to word this is the concept of falling into the comparison trap.

Don't get me wrong. I'm extremely competitive. I'm one of six siblings that all love to play games and compete. But as Christ-followers, our walk with God cannot be treated like a competition. If you find yourself trying to measure up to those around you, I promise you that your eyes are going to be so transfixed on other people that, before you know it, you won't even be able to see God right in front of you or hear His direction for your life. Our goal on this earth is not to compete or become a better Christian than the person down the street from us. Rather, our goal is to love God with everything that we are and to exist solely to see His will be carried out. Then, as an overflow and extension of loving God with all that we are, we love those around us, His children, as much as we love ourselves (shoutout Love More, Worry Less). If you're living out your faith in the realm of a competition, then you're in complete violation of what God's desire is for your life.

Trust me when I say I've been there. In fact, I lived in this camp of Christianity for far too long. I battle against it sometimes to this very day. When I got into high school and people around me started partying, sleeping around, and doing other types of things, I would pull the holier-than-thou card on the daily. (Only in my mind—don't worry, I never did it in person. Even though, according to Jesus, this is the same thing. So I'm just as guilty.) I'd be struggling with my own sins of lust, comparison, and the battle of anxiety, and then I would tell myself, *Well, I'm not as bad as those people, so God will probably focus more on their sins anyway.* Yikes. Anyone have a Bible nearby? Can you see if this type of theology exists anywhere in it?

Oh yeah, that's right. It doesn't.

The danger of trying to measure up to others is either finding yourself in the comparison trap of feeling like you're never going to be as good as those you feel like are ahead of you. Or you may find yourself stuck in the lie that your sins aren't as bad as other people's, so you can just continue living how you want to. Both of these ways of life contradict how God wants us to live. In fact, comparison is a very real and very clever tool that the enemy uses against us. If he can sneak his way into our minds and convince us that our sin isn't as bad as we think, then as far as he's concerned, that's a victory for his team.

God doesn't call you to measure up to others. He calls you to step into the unique calling and anointing that He's set before you. That's right. Read that statement again if you need to. No one else. You!

Don't live your faith from a scarcity mindset. That's downright dangerous. Sometimes, we can adopt this idea from the world that if we aren't selfish with God and who He is, then the best calling or blessings or miracles may go to someone else, so we better just keep Him to ourselves. Well, by doing this, you're robbing a dying world of the truth they desperately need, and you're creating a box for God that He's way too big to live in. Trust me, there's plenty of Him to go around. What He's set before you to experience has been laid out and determined before you were even born when He called you in your mother's womb and knew the amount of hairs on your head. After all, He's the Ultimate Designer, Architect, and Creator behind your life. (Just check out Luke 12:7 and Jeremiah 1:5.)

This conversation about comparing ourselves to others has a multitude of layers to it as well, all of which are compromising and dangerous to your faith. Let's start with the surface level. Each and every one of us has compared ourselves to another person based solely on looks. You wish you looked more like them, dressed more like them, had more friends like them, got more likes like them. Whatever it may be for you, you've been there. And would you like an indicator that your faith has taken up residence inside the comparison trap? I'd like you to think about how you think, talk, and look at other people. Oh yeah, I'm going there. Some people's feelings may be hurt by this.

If you're someone who judges, gossips, and talks bad about people around you constantly, the bad news I have for you is it's because you're stuck in the realm of comparison. You're well aware of the fact that there are people better than you, so you single out others that you've decided aren't. You know that you're insecure, so you find people that you can mask your insecurity with by talking down on them. It's easy to know where someone's heart is at just based on the way they talk, joke, use, and treat others. Someone who needs the safety net of comparing themselves to others realizes that there are people above them, and they, therefore, prey on people below them. This is also a direct violation of when Jesus commands us to love others as ourselves, and I'm not sure about you, but I don't want to contradict the Savior of the world.

You've got the disease of comparison that is ravaging the message of Jesus if these words are striking a cord right now. Stop trying to measure up and consequently creating a group of people who, in your mind, will never measure up to you.

Now, I know what you're thinking, so I've prepared myself for it. If you're someone who struggles with gossip and judging others, I know the justification that you'll present in your mind goes something like this: "Well, I don't judge people because I don't love them. Some people are just harder to love! There are some people that require a little extra grace, and sometimes, I need to let off steam with my spouse or co-workers! The people I'm talking bad about will never know, so, therefore, no harm, no foul."

Nice try. But I'm afraid that idea doesn't exist in the gospel, and it does so much damage to our goal of loving God and loving others. Not only this, but we are also commanded as Christ-followers to guard our hearts and minds from anything that isn't loving or honoring to God or other people (Philippians 4:8). Yes, even the thoughts you think need to be clean of hateful things! God sees what others don't. Humble yourself and realize that you, too, are a product of God's grace and forgiveness; therefore, no excuse is good enough not to extend that same grace and forgiveness to others. Yes, even the ones that push your buttons a little bit extra. In the chapters to follow, we're going to get into the idea of judgment and how lucky we are that the story is a little bit unfair in our direction. So, just buckle up.

This conversation also applies to our relationship with God. We can't measure up to God. Maybe that sounds like a basic concept to you, but truly get that in your mind. There is not and there will never be someone or something like God. And part of this process that we've walked so far is accepting our brokenness, fighting against competition with others, and now humbly submitting ourselves to the fact that we are not God. As a matter of fact, we're very far from it (which we're going to look at in the next chapter).

Here's the deal: you're small. We're small! The human race

is small. For those of you with raging muscles who just read that line, you may not be physically small, and I'm not implying that, so don't hurt me. Please. The smallness I'm talking about is grander than physical stature.

Don't believe me? Wherever you are right now, I want you to look outside. Look up into the sky at the sun or moon and stars. I want you to think about how far away those things are. But let's not stop there. I want you to think about how, past those things, there is an endless galaxy that contains planets that have never been seen nor inhabited. Matter we'll never know about. Things that would blow our minds if we were able to look upon their beauty.

Now, bring it back down to earth and look around you at the neighborhood or city or countryside that you're in. I want you to take in how the land around you just goes on for miles and miles and miles. And that land eventually turns into different towns, cities, states, countries, continents, cultures, people groups, existences.

We could go on forever, but here's the deal. You, my friend, are small.

And that's a *very* good thing.

We're small. Some would even argue that we're borderline insignificant when compared to the vastness and wonder of the world and galaxy around us.

Yet God calls you *His*. God desires to know you on a personal, first name, basis. God calls you fearfully and wonderfully made (Psalm 139:14). God decided that He loved you so much that He wanted to send His only Son to die a painful death for you (John 3:16).

The same God who created every single thing that you see (and everything you don't) wanted you to play a supporting role in His story. In fact, He's written a unique story for you based on your skills and abilities and circumstances. But it won't come if you're still hoping to be cast as the main character.

Do you think that, in some way, you can measure up to this God? To the most creative, intelligent, beautiful Artist of all time? There's no way!

Exactly. So stop trying.

If you carry the mindset that you're supposed to measure up to this one true God, you will soon become crushed and overwhelmed by that task. You'll find yourself simply defeated by the fact that nothing you could ever do will get you any closer to measuring up to this God.

So stop!

Stop attempting to measure up to this God that is before all things, in all things, and the Maker of all things. You are a byproduct of God's genius, and even though you are small in this vast world, you're the only thing in creation made in His image! (Read Genesis 1:27 again.) This doesn't mean that you're supposed to be God by any means, but it does mean that this all-powerful God created you to be His child. And that's a reason to celebrate.

But the only way to truly come to terms with this beautiful fact of our history is to humbly lay down our pride and submit to the fact that God is in charge of everything, and therefore, we are not.

God is the Maker of all things, and you are the lucky benefactor of His creativity. God is the ultimate standard of perfection, and you are a small, broken image of Him. Do not attempt to measure up to Him, or you'll find yourself crushed under the perfection that comes with who God is and who you were never created to be. You weren't cast in God's grand drama of humanity to play the perfect character, so pick up a different script. Instead, lay your life down before a God that has earned the victory for you. Whoops, I've said too much. We're really heating up now.

✞

SOMETHING IS MISSING

You made it.

Time to go home. Today was one of those days that felt like an entire week rolled into a couple hours. But, regardless of how much the day dragged by, you finished your to-do list of work for the day and the sweet reward of a night at home is now waiting for you.

As you pack your things up, you see a few of your friends that you used to spend a lot of time with making plans to hang out together, but at this point, it isn't much of a surprise that you're no longer invited to these types of things. They never have to say it, and none of them ever have, but you know it's because their parents don't want them associating themselves with the one who has "*that* older brother."

So, you get your things together, head outside, and start walking home by yourself.

As of the last few weeks, it's become a normality for you to do this walk by yourself. And even though some days are extremely lonely, you remind yourself that this is the best time to do some thinking. Complete silence and peace of mind has become an unexpected benefit of being an outcast. So, you begin to think about things from God, to what's for dinner, to your family situation.

But unlike other days, the topic of your family is taking up a lot of your headspace on this particularly lonely walk home. Your mind continues to turn back to it. You realize that you haven't seen your brother since he stormed out on Saturday morning, and your parents haven't talked much about him in front of you either. And today is Tuesday.

What in the world is going on?

As you continue to walk down this road in your mind, you're led back to the place of God's involvement in all of this. Except this time, you find yourself heartbroken. *Is my brother really unforgivable? Is it true that he's eternally lost and can never be found? Is it true that his actions have rendered him completely and utterly useless in the eyes of God? Am I useless, too? I've made mistakes. We all do, right? God, how come his are so much worse than my own?*

Before you know it, you find yourself at your front door. You head inside and journey up to your bedroom. Upon entering your room, you collapse on the edge of your bed, and the emotions finally flood in. The pain. The sadness. The heartbreak. The weight of the questions parading through your mind. The only response you can muster is to cry.

Why is this the situation your family has found itself in? Why is this the hand that you've been dealt? Where is God in all this pain and this mess? Will it ever get better?

As all these emotions, questions, and doubts flood your mind, you're reminded of the times that you and your brother had growing up. At this point in your life, it seems like a memory far off in the distance. The laughter. The games. The times spent together. What has messed it all up so badly?

But the thing that makes this messy situation so much messier for you is the fact that despite all of the things your brother has done, he's always been there for you. As little kids, you developed a symbol with him—a sign that everything was going to be okay. The wink. It's so simple, and yet, it was a bond made between siblings that could not be broken, no matter the circumstance or situation.

Suddenly, you're swept away by the memories and moments of pure joy and nostalgia that you two shared growing up: the inside jokes, the holidays, the true companionship that only comes from having someone that shares the same blood as you. As these memories continue to flow, so do the tears.

But suddenly, your door is pushed open slightly.

"Hey," you hear a voice whisper.

Assuming it's your parents, you quickly wipe your tears and sniffles in order to avoid any conversation about what had been going on. You don't want to make the burden any heavier on them than it already is. Only, it's not either of your parents.

It's your brother.

"Oh my goodness!" you exclaim. "What are you doing here?"

"What do you mean what am I doing here? This is my house, you know?" your brother responds sarcastically.

"Oh, be quiet. Where in the world have you been? And not only that, but what in the world did you do? Mom and Dad are really upset this time," you explain.

"Don't worry about it. They're always going to be upset with me. It doesn't matter what I do or don't do. I'll never be able to earn their acceptance at this point," he scoffs.

"Well, you always have mine, even if that's not true for Mom and Dad. I'll always love you, no matter what," you shoot back.

"That's refreshing to hear. You know that I love you, too, even when I run off or do things that seem otherwise," he says.

"Why do you do these things that are going to get you in trouble, time and time again? You do realize that people are starting to really notice, and it's affecting our entire family's reputation, right? Even my own friends stopped hanging out with me at school! Can you just tell me why?" you inquire.

After a few moments of silence, your brother's words cut through faintly, almost inaudibly, "It's who I am. I'm broken—after so long of not being fully loved or accepted by everyone around you, you'll do anything just to feel better. To feel accepted. To feel like you have a purpose. I hope you never have to feel that way. But I do. What started off as a few bad decisions has become my identity. Everyone has seen me this way for so long, I might as well accept it, too."

As he finishes speaking, you both begin to cry silently. It's in moments like these between the two of you that you are reminded how human you brother is and how his pain is very evident through his actions. Your heart breaks even further, and it's as if time has stopped just for a moment as you both cry. What else can be said in a moment like this?

Suddenly, he stands up and heads toward the door. He clears

his throat, turns around to face you, and says, "Anyway, I have to go, but I'm really, really thankful for you and how I never have to doubt your love for me."

"Why did you come in here?" you ask, curious as to what the intent was of this conversation, because knowing your brother, it sure wasn't for a cry sesh.

Quieting his voice back down once again, he responds, "Well—to be honest, I'm involved with some really bad people right now. That's why Mom and Dad have been so secretive about it with you. I really messed up this time, and they're threatening to hurt you guys if I don't do what they ask," he answers.

It's as if you can't breathe as you listen to the words that leave his mouth. *What does he mean "bad people?" They want to hurt our family? What has he done?*

You stutter and attempt to find the words for what feels like a couple minutes, and almost involuntarily, you whisper the question, "What kinds of things are they asking you to do?" You're not even sure you want to hear the response to such a question, but your mouth had other plans.

"Now, that is an answer that I definitely cannot share," he chuckles and continues on. "I'll be back in a few days, but I have to leave right now, and I wanted to make sure I saw you first so that you knew everything was going to be okay."

As he backs out of your room, he winks as he closes the door.

You do the same in return. As always.

Everything is going to be okay.
Right?

☩

A little bit earlier, I referenced the disease that is running rampant inside the walls of the church, and its name is comparison.

Just for a moment, I want to come full circle and bring this conversation back into light.

Comparison will rob you of your God-given purpose, identity, and design faster than you can even blink. One day, you could be awakened to the fact that you were named, called, and set apart by God before you were even born, and in the very next breath, find yourself stuck in the quicksand of comparison. It's dangerous. It's insulting to the God that created you. It's a silent killer of our faith.

Stop trying to measure up.

Maybe it's time to accept the fact that you were never meant to or, better yet, that it's impossible for you to. You may feel like you're above those around you, but in reality, you're only fooling yourself, walking ever deeper into the enemy's trap.

Comparison is a dangerous game.

This is the problem that our culture has brought into our faith. Just look around you! You want that job? Compete for it. You want that guy or girl? Compete for them. You want those followers on social media? Compete to show that you're worth it. You want money? Compete for that raise or promotion. The list goes on. And it is downright overwhelming.

So, naturally, because this is the way that our world is telling us to think, we've allowed these ideals to seep into and become intertwined with the story of God. We hold these misconceptions in our minds—that if we want a place in Heaven, we have to compete for it. This is destroying what Jesus wants for us.

CLUE #2 -
IF YOUR GOAL IS TO MEASURE UP, YOU'RE GOING TO FALL SHORT EVERY SINGLE TIME (SO CHANGE YOUR GOAL).

Chapter 3

IF PERFECTION IS THE STANDARD

I'll be honest. I'm a hopeless romantic. I just *love* love. I always have, and I always will. It doesn't take much for a sappy love story to make me emotional or a movie to tug at my heartstrings. That means my wife, Lexi, sometimes has to deal with the emotional, romantic mess that is me.

And a part of being in a relationship with a lovebird like me is that I give compliments. A lot. Sometimes I compliment so often that the things I'm saying lose their power. My compliments have sometimes been so frequent that they have become commonplace in the language of our marriage. This means that, instead of saying things like, "Hey, you're beautiful," to Lexi, I've begun to create more power with my words by telling her specifically what I think is beautiful about her. If I can get specific about the compliment, it can offset the commonplace nature of my words, which, in turn, makes them actually mean something. Let me explain, though, how I came to this realization.

There was one time in the first couple months of our marriage that I'll never forget. In a single sentence, Lexi changed my perception about something that I had been doing for years. There was an expectation that I was creating with my verbiage that I didn't even realize, and it centered on the word "perfect."

We were sitting on the couch one night watching TV, and I looked over at Lexi and began to think about how lucky I was to be married to my best friend (literally, we've been best friends since fifth grade). Beginning to be overwhelmed by the feeling of love that I had for her, I said, "Wow—you're just so perfect." It's a pretty typical compliment, right?

You see, for me, this was something that I would say to Lexi every once in a while over the years that we had been dating. It wasn't that I literally thought she had no imperfections (she would say the same about me, don't worry), but it was an expression of the fact that she was so perfect for me. She was what I had always been searching for in a partner.

But in this particular moment, after I had shared my feelings about her perfection, she looked over at me with an inquisitive look on her face.

Oh no. What did I say wrong? I thought to myself.

After a couple moments of what seemed like intense thought on her part, she replied, "Thank you. But you don't have to call me perfect. Honestly, I know I'm not, because none of us are, and when you call me perfect, it creates an expectation that I'll never be able to reach."

Snap. Mind blown. That was brilliant.

At that moment, it hit me so hard. When we offer these simple acknowledgments of perfection to our significant others—children, influential people, and whoever else—we may be communicating a standard or an expectation that simply can never be reached.

My wife is so good at moments like these. In fact, she has taught me so much about life, love, and God simply by the way she lives in and sees the world. She speaks truth sometimes in very simple yet pointed and awesome ways. I may take time and whole handfuls of words to try communicating the same exact idea. We are so different, and yet the way that we come together and sharpen each other is one of my favorite things about our friendship and marriage so far. Anyway, I better stop before I get emotional. I'm such a cry baby.

From that moment forward, I began to shift my language. Instead of claiming that Lexi was perfect, I began to say things like, "You're so perfect for me," as well as compliments of that nature, which helps me communicate what I've wanted her to hear from me the whole time.

So what about this standard of perfection? Is it truly damaging? Well, it depends on how you look at it. Let's look at how the standard of perfection can be damaging if we aren't careful, starting with the standard that we may be holding for other people.

This is a tricky one. And dare I say, it's humbling to admit that we do it all the time, myself included. We frequently hold those around us to a standard of perfection without even realizing it. Just think about some people who are close to you in your own life. What happens if they mess up? Fall short? Have a bad day? Speak too fast? What is your reaction toward them? Even the reaction that you have in your head that no one else will ever see—is it graceful, is it kind, is it loving? This reaction to those around us is extremely revealing of what our hearts are actually saying. This reaction can very quickly reveal that we hold an unfair standard of perfection for those around us. How dare I say such a thing?

Well—think about your thoughts. What an interesting thing to ask of someone—to think of their thoughts. What is this, *Inception*? Leonardo DiCaprio, where you at?

How many times a day do you mess up? Fall short? Speak or think too fast? And yet, odds are, you don't immediately call yourself out and demand forgiveness or for amends to be made. Yet we do it to other people all the time. This is an immediate red flag indicating that we are holding those around us to a standard of perfection that they simply cannot meet—one that we don't even expect from ourselves. And this standard of other people that we set has a byproduct. Its name?

Judgment.

And, boy oh boy, do we live in a world run by judgment, or what!

If you have some free time, go ahead and do a Google search on some verses about judging others. It's safe to say that it's going to be a hard pill to swallow. It's not easy to continue rationalizing how we talk, gossip, and judge other people once we look at the biblical standard for it. Long story short: if you judge, you're going to be judged. Need I say more? Okay, fine, I'll say one more thing: gossip makes the short list of seven things that God hates. Yikes. Just read Proverbs 6:16-19 if you don't believe me.

Now, there is a time and place for correction, rebuking, speaking up, and things of that nature. I'm not at all saying that all forms of correction are judgment—not even close. Otherwise, Christianity would become like the Wild Wild West, and we'd all be able to do whatever we wanted. This is just not how it was designed to work.

What we say and think about other people really matters to God. What you think in your heart matters just as much as your actions in the eyes of Jesus. A lot more on this in this next chapter.

But maybe you're reading this, and you're in a position where you don't find yourself holding others to a standard of perfection that much. That's awesome. No, seriously. That's fantastic, and I want to challenge you to keep it up and fight against the urge to speak ill of other people.

So, maybe this conversation on the standard of perfection falls more on your shoulders. You hold yourself to this standard. What other people do in your life and how they do it affects you, sure, but the weight that you carry is based on your own actions. When you mess up or fall short, your soul feels it. Your bones ache.

Wow. I've been there. I'm still there. I can't even elaborate how much I feel those words that I just wrote. But can I be honest? There is a healthy and unhealthy way to hold yourself to a standard of perfection. Let's take a quick look at both.

Let's start with the unhealthy side.

If you're someone who holds yourself to a standard of perfection in everything that you do, then you don't allow space for mistakes, growth, trials, and experimenting. You are only setting yourself up for disappointment and deep pain. In fact, you will find yourself becoming a slave to your performance and work that will surely fall away as seasons change, success comes and goes, and doors open and shut. Please hear me when I say this: this is not the way to live your life.

When people find themselves attempting to live up to an unhealthy standard of perfection, where they are always chasing more and running after bigger and better things, it can unlock a very ugly side of our humanity called discontentment. This is a human feeling that can damage and decrease our freedom, joy, and humanity.

A few months before I started to write this book, I was stuck in a season of discontentment. Like very, very stuck. I was going to work every day, doing what needed to be done, and wrestling in the back of my mind because I wasn't happy where God had me. And don't get me wrong, I love what I do. It gets me out of bed and sometimes keeps me up at night. I love it.

But that doesn't mean that the devil hadn't pulled up a seat at the table in my mind and began to whisper negative thoughts to me. The worst part? I thought this voice was God's. I was strongly convinced that God was planting seeds of discontentment in my heart to show me that something else was on the horizon.

It got to a point where those who were close to me knew something was up. My wife would ask me about it. My boss noticed that my attitude wasn't great. And even in my own head, I was growing less and less joyful as each day passed.

Finally, one day, a friend of mine worked up the courage to call me out on it. And thank the Lord that he did.

"What's up?" I asked, slightly confused at what was happening.

"Are you doing okay today?" he asked back.

"Yeah! I'm good. Fine. Busy day as usual," I responded with a smile on my face.

"You don't have to lie to me of all people. I know that you're not okay. So what is it?" he responded.

Isn't it funny how some people can cut through all of the junk and ask the questions that really matter? Man, I want to be one of those people. Jesus was one of those people.

I opened up in that moment and began sharing my frustrations that I had been having. About work. About being stuck. About being confused about what God wanted from me. The list went on and on and on.

After a few moments of my complaints, he finally responded and said that it sounded like I was feeling discontent.

"That's exactly what I'm feeling!" I answered. I was relieved that it made sense and that he understood what I was feeling in that moment.

Then he said, "I'm afraid that's a human feeling. That discontentment is a result of sin, whether it be yours or someone else's. And from everything you've said and even the things I see in your job, I have a feeling it's your sin."

Well okay then.

Who gives you the right?

Despite the initial feelings of anger and annoyance, I knew he was right. God wasn't planting seeds of discontentment. The enemy was. And I was allowing those seeds to be watered. I was even allowing them to grow!

You know what God was planting and is still trying to plant in all of us?

Seeds of faithfulness and obedience.

Can we honestly say that we're watering those?

You see, when we hold ourselves to a high standard of perfection and are always looking forward to the next big thing in our lives or what the future holds, we absolutely lose sight of the now—of the people, opportunities, and mission that God has right in front of our eyes.

God is calling you to be faithful—to serve Him where you are, to use your gifts, abilities, calling, job, money, and life to serve and honor Him.

Does He expect ultimate perfection from you? Well, if He required it, then there'd only be one person in Heaven with Him right now, and His name is Jesus.

But God does expect faithfulness. And obedience. And the willingness to say, "Yes," when He calls you to something. Not only that, but He is expecting you to do *something*—anything that brings Him glory. Sometimes, we get so overwhelmed trying to be perfect that we're too paralyzed to take a step.

Don't become a slave to the standard of perfection that you've set in your mind. Welcome to the life of a human being: broken, searching, incomplete.

Also, you are simultaneously loved, forgiven, accepted, and called. Whoops, I keep doing that. I have to slow down. I don't want to give the secret away just yet.

But this conversation on the standard we set for ourselves isn't over just yet. I strongly believe there is a healthy side to this conversation as well.

If the only answer to this question was, "Well, you'll never be perfect, so don't expect to be!" I think we'd end up with a lot of aimless, unchanged, set-in-their-ways Christ-followers, which is very far from the standard we're called to according to Scripture.

If that was the end of the story, then how can we justify Matthew 5:48, which reads, "But you are to be perfect, even as your Father in Heaven is perfect"?

Hmm. So our conversation isn't over just yet. Does God really expect us to be perfect? To be like Him? How? And where the in the world do we even start?

In a couple chapters, I want to get into this in-depth, so we are going to do just that. But what we have to understand as a foundation is that the God of the Bible is perfect. God can do no wrong. He is a just, fair, loving, righteous, awesome, huge, perfect God. Not only this, but He is holy. In short, that means He is set apart and above the rest of creation. Not only this, but even with all of these characteristics of God, He's also good. That's a part of His character as well, and I think we forget it.

This perfect, holy, set apart, just, good God cannot exist with evil, sin, and darkness. That's what we are.

Which means something is missing.

And we should be thankful for it.

Trust me, we are so close to revealing what this something is, and I cannot wait for you to experience it.

But for now, that's the point that needs to be clear in order to go forward. The God of the Bible is perfect, and He requires a standard of perfection in order for us to be in relationship with Him. This is why there is a certain standard of perfection in our own lives that is healthy.

Let me put it this way: for those of you reading who have a relationship with Jesus, I hope that you understand that your main overarching goal on planet earth is to be like Jesus in everything that you do. Every single day. Every single moment. Our goal is to dive deep into the example of Jesus that is left for us in the pages of the Bible, do our best to walk in His footsteps, submit ourselves to His way of life, and commit to following Him every day while allowing the Holy Spirit to carry this out as we rely on Him.

Easy peasy, right? No big deal.

I mean, after all, Jesus is only the perfect Son of God, who never committed a sin and fought off temptation by having Scripture memorized in His heart, and not to mention it, but He also walked on water, casted out demons, brought dead friends back to life, healed the sick, was murdered, and raised Himself from the dead.

Oh, that's all? That's the job description? Sweet, I'll get on that right now.

Okay, maybe it's not so easy. Maybe it's a little bit overwhelming to look at the life of Jesus and attempt to be like Him in our world.

Exactly.

There's your goal. Your mission. Your purpose. Your drive. No one has ever been able to do it perfectly since Him, and it's a biblical fact that no one ever will. Which means we have pretty big shoes to fill. It means the goal will always be before us. It means that this healthy standard of perfection will create a daily, moment-by-moment, intense focus and commitment to be like Jesus more and more, every day of our lives.

Something that has really been on my heart lately that I think is extremely relevant to add to this conversation is the fact that God loves you too much to let you stay where you are. If you're in the church world, you've probably heard a statement like this before, but wow, it's so true. God loves you so much—more than anyone else will. And He is also the perfect standard of love, which means He is the perfect example of the fact that love is not acceptance. When you believe in Jesus and start a relationship with Him, He goes to work! Jesus is redeeming, changing, shaping, working, and refining your life and heart. If you started following God at some point and you are exactly the same now as you were then, then it's extremely possible that you were never following God in the first place. Maybe the god of your heart is just you.

God works in our hearts and sets us on a course to be more like His Son, Jesus, so that our original design to be image bearers of Him can come to light through our stories, actions, and hearts.

Now, we're getting somewhere.

You see, this standard of perfection that we set for ourselves can be healthy if it's tethered to the person of Jesus. We realize that we'll never be perfect, but we serve a God who is. We make the switch from unhealthy to healthy when we realize that following Jesus doesn't mean we'll automatically be perfect, but it does mean that we have a daily and constant path set before us that can fuel every waking moment of our human existence.

And let me end this section by clarifying this: this standard that God requires isn't just about actions. As we all know, we are going to fail in terms of actions every single day. What I'm saying is that when you begin to walk with Jesus, you undergo heart surgery, and a changed heart is going to lead to a changed person. God doesn't expect perfection from you, but He's called you to live a life of righteousness and holiness (which are not the same as *being* perfect). God is the only perfect being that exists, but each and every one of us is called toward a life of being transformed into the image of Him, more and more, day by day.

Perfection is a standard that can't be met. The path toward righteousness (our morality being like God) and holiness (being set apart by God) are things that are walked every day. That's why the Bible often says we "become" these things.

You aren't expected to be perfect in your actions, but you are called to progress into the image of Jesus, more and more, every day.

Paul's words in Romans 5:1-5 help a lot with these ideas if you want to go a little deeper.

☧

Knock. Knock. Knock.

Another Sabbath. Another morning where you're woken up before you need to be. You fight off feelings of anger from being awakened too early yet again. But before you know it, the real fact of the matter rushes into your mind.

Could that be him? you think to yourself. It's been a couple weeks since you last saw your brother. In fact, the conversation that you and he had in your room was the last time you've even heard from him.

But everything was going to be okay. Right?

Suddenly, you hear your mom begin sobbing from downstairs: not just any type of sobbing but wailing. It's to the point of you being able to hear every inhale and shaky breath from her. You jump out of bed, not even fully dressed, and run down the stairs to find both of your parents standing at the front door with two military officials on the other side.

Wait, what?

Your parents notice you standing there, and your dad reaches out his hand as if to invite you down to where they're standing. You aren't able to make out your mom's eyes because she is buried in your dad's chest, continuing to sob.

You slowly walk down the remaining stairs and join your parents in an embrace tighter than you've ever received from them.

What in the world is going on? you think to yourself.

One of the officials speaks up from outside the front door and asks, "Would you like me to fill them in on what has happened with your son?"

"No, that's okay," your father responds rather harshly. "We can handle it ourselves."

"Totally understandable. Well, then, we'll see you in a few weeks. I'm sorry that we had to break the news to you this morning on your Sabbath, but the news was simply too urgent. God bless," the official responds.

As your parents shut the door, your mind is racing with a

million thoughts. In fact, thoughts are overlapping each other because of how fast your mind is moving. You find yourself asking in your head: *Why were two military men sent to our house? Is he dead? What did he do now? Why will we see them in a couple weeks? Where is my brother?*

You notice that your father has begun crying as well now that the three of you are alone. You can't remember the last time you've seen him cry. In fact, you could count the amount of times you've seen your dad be even slightly emotional on one hand. This must be bad—like really, really bad.

After a couple minutes of your mind moving a million miles an hour, you become unable to bear the sound of your own thoughts any longer. You forcefully pull away from their embrace and demand, "What happened? Where is he?"

"Um—let's go ahead and sit down somewhere, so we can talk about what needs to happen now," your father says while drying his tears and pulling himself together.

Both of your parents begin to walk toward the kitchen, still embracing, leaving you standing there alone by the door.

"No!" you shout. "No. No. No. Just answer me. Please! I'm a part of this family, and I love him more than you two ever have, so please, just tell me what is going on!"

A little bit shocked by the statement that you just made, your parents make eye contact, and your father clears his throat, returning his eyes back to you. "Well—this may sound cliché, but there is no easy way to put this. We know you love your brother very much. And you've always been there for him through everything that he's done. We love him, too, and we hope that he knows that. But he is lost—unbelievably lost—and we don't think that he will ever be able to find forgiveness from God again—"

"Okay, okay, that's all great. What did he do?" you cut in.

Your dad continues, "Well—um—it seems to us that he's been involved with a really bad crowd for a while now—one that has ramped up his usual schemes of general neighborhood disturbances to more serious crimes—crimes that he could lose his life over—"

"What did he do?!" you yell.

"He killed someone," your dad blurts out. The statement came out so dry and empty that it took a moment for your mind to even catch up with what was just said.

The entire atmosphere of the room shifts. Both of your parents break out in tears once again, and your dad's face looks like he could throw up just from saying those words out loud. It's as if the entire world has stopped spinning and fallen apart all with those three words.

You find yourself unable to breathe for a moment. The pressure in your chest is extremely tight and borderline suffocating. It's as if all of your worst fears and deepest realizations are crashing in on you all at once. Every doubt and fear that you've ever had about your brother was true. He really was as bad as people said he was.

Not only this, but for the first time you find yourself stepping across the line in your own mind, thinking that he may never be able to find God again. It's as if all of the walls and structures of your ideals that you've built after years of watching him walk down this road are all falling apart, crashing into each other, and leaving nothing in their place but chaos and destruction.

How could God let this happen? you ask yourself, and for the first time in your life, the thought of God brings a bad taste into your mouth. For the first time, you wonder if this God that you've always been told to believe in is anything other than a horrible, mean, unloving being in the sky. *After all*, you think to yourself, *if this God is anything like what is taught in Sunday school, and if He actually loved us, how could He let something like this happen?*

CLUE #3 -
A PERFECT GOD CANNOT EXIST WITH SIN. BUT THAT'S WHO WE ARE. HOW CAN WE REACH THE LEVEL OF GOD'S APPROVAL? WE NEED SOMETHING TO BE ADDED TO THE EQUATION. OR SOMETHING TO GO MISSING FROM THE RECORD.

Chapter 4

THE MURDERER IN EACH OF US

"So, you're telling me that God forgives me, Donald Trump, Joe Biden, and Hitler the same way?"

Wow. Well, good morning to you, too, I thought to myself as a fifth grade boy asked this question bright and early on a Sunday morning.

I had been leading a series with these middle school students over the last couple weeks on forgiveness, and I arrived at the fun part in the conversation where I brought up the fact that God's forgiveness doesn't have a scale like we often think it does. In fact, it doesn't even have a limit. If we truly claim to believe that God's forgiveness isn't based on what we've done but rather on who He is, then we also have to adopt a scenario such as the one that I presented to these fifth and sixth graders. It went a little bit like this.

"Okay, so, if God's forgiveness is freely available to everyone and what determines whether someone receives this forgiveness isn't what they've done but what's in their heart when they ask God for forgiveness, then God's forgiveness cannot be based on a scale! It doesn't take more or less forgiveness based on who the person is or what they've done. The mind-blowing part of this is that someone who cheats on a math test is forgiven the same way as a serial killer who truly believes in Jesus and asks for forgiveness after everything they've done—even though our human minds want to tell us this is wrong!"

After delivering this statement at the end of my message for that morning, one of the fifth graders in the class shoots up his hand and blurts out, "So, you're telling me that God forgives me, Donald Trump, Joe Biden and Hitler the same way?"

See, the question that this little boy asked is fantastic. I really want to write a sermon series called, "So You Think You're Better Than Hitler?" but my wife told me it's a little bit too forceful. But I want to make his question the focus of this chapter. Except I don't want you to think about the people on his list, necessarily, but rather, I want you to think of someone (or a couple people) that you think are absolutely horrible. Maybe they've done terrible things, or their reputation is rough, or they're notorious for being hated. It doesn't matter the reason for why your mind went to this person or people, but I want you to think about them right now.

Okay, you got it? Are you ready for this?

God loves them, too.

God forgives them, too.

God created them, too.

God sent His Son for them, too.

You're just as broken as they are.

That may be easy to accept on the surface and go on about your life, but I'm afraid that, for the sake of this book and in order to truly find what's missing, you're going to have to accept this truth as absolute truth. You need to live by it as well. The example I always use for this, due to the fact that he is universally evil, is Adolf Hitler.

Because of the very nature of sin, God's unconditional love, and God's incomprehensible forgiveness, we have to accept that someone as horrible and vile as Hitler could also end up in the paradise of Heaven. I know this is hypothetical, but if, in the final moments of Hitler's life, consider what would happen if he had a radical heart change and came to terms with the fact that he was incredibly broken and evil because of his actions and heart. Then, in that moment, he prayed to God with sincere motives—something like this: "I am so incredibly broken, and nothing about my life would render me worthy to inherit eternal life. But I was wrong in everything that I did, and I've come to realize that you are real, and you sent your Son to die for my brokenness. Because of this, even though I don't deserve it, I want to ask for forgiveness because your grace isn't based on my actions, but who you are." If this had actually happened, we would have to believe that he would be saved. But not if he was doing this for show or for any false motives other than true, unmerited repentance. Need reference for such a wild idea? Dig into Acts 2:21, Romans 10:13, or 10:9 to get started.

If you find yourself disagreeing with me at this point of the chapter, that's okay! Sometimes, an idea like this that contradicts our human concepts of right and wrong, fair and unfair, or good and evil can be hard to process. I want to challenge you to keep reading as we unpack this ideal from the basis of Scripture. I promise you that what we're going to find is different than what you may want to believe. What you may find is the fact that in each one of us lies a murderer. And I didn't come up with this idea. It's straight from the mouth of Jesus Himself.

In the middle of Jesus' most famous sermon called the Sermon on the Mount, He begins speaking to the crowd about some misconceptions that they've had in regard to practices and ideas that they've grown up with. Multiple times in this section of His sermon, you'll read the phrase, "You have heard it said… but I say…" The reason why this section is extremely important for

Jesus' ministry (and probably why He ended up being murdered) is because He was shedding light on religious practices that people were using to disguise and hide their motives and hearts that were very far from God.

So, in this particular section that we will look at for a moment, I want to get you to see that there's a murderer inside of you, too. Turn your attention to Matthew chapter 5 for a moment. Let's pick it up starting in verse 21 (all from the NLT translation).

"'You have heard that our ancestors were told, 'You must not murder. If you commit murder, you are subject to judgment.'"

I would imagine that, at this point, Jesus' hearers didn't have too much to complain about (hopefully neither do we). It would be kind of funny though if a murderer was in the crowd, and they shouted something like, "We need to crucify this man immediately! Cancel Him! He's taking away my truth! I murder other people for fun! Other people's bodies, my choice!"

I seriously apologize for that. Let's just move on.

What I'm getting at is the fact that Jesus hasn't dropped a shocker on anyone listening yet. The mandate not to murder someone has been around since the Old Testament, and we know that murder is universally wrong. That's what I love most about these "You have heard it said… but I say…" statements because Jesus is almost baiting His listeners to agree with Him as He begins, when they find themselves on an equal playing field. But as we know, Jesus is just getting started, and He believes there's a whole other side to these commands. So He continues in verse 22:

"But I say, if you are even angry with someone, you are subject to judgment! If you call someone an idiot, you are in danger of being brought before the court. And if you curse someone, you are in danger of the fires of Hell."

Jesus, what the on earth was that, man?

We were with you in the first half with the no murdering thing, but now you're trying to get us to believe that if we're even angry with someone, that's the same as murdering them? What kind of thing are you trying to sell here?

See, this type of bold statement wasn't uncommon for Jesus' ministry. He often spins ideals that the people held tightly to in a new way, bringing God's underlying truth to light. This is just one example of many.

What Jesus is trying to get us to understand here is that, in the Kingdom of God, what happens in our hearts matters just as much as what we do. This means that, in the eyes of God, even thinking ill or hating someone is the same as murdering them; it just happens in your heart.

So, you do have a murderer living inside of you. Go ahead and get familiar with each other. There's one in all of us. Exchange pleasantries, talk about your highs and lows, do an icebreaker. Whatever you need to do to get introduced to each other properly is fine by me.

You—whoever you are—reading these words right now, with all of your mistakes, mess-ups, and shortcomings, are just as guilty and unworthy of God's forgiveness as the next person with their mistakes, mess-ups, and shortcomings. And I can firmly say that without needing to know the details of your sin or how bad it may seem because what I do know is how good our Savior is and how vast His forgiveness is for us. And that's enough for me to come to terms with the murderer inside of me (the pain, brokenness, and sin) and allow it to die to the Savior who was murdered for me, even though I'm the one who deserved it.

✟

What followed the bombshell moment in your family was numbness. There's no better word to describe the way that it all felt. Lifeless. Empty. Numb.

The explosion happened on a Saturday morning, which meant

that by the next day, you found yourself dressed up and in the synagogue for Sunday service. As you walked to the service in your family of three, you noticed a peculiar vibe coming from the people in your neighborhood who were walking the same direction: whispers, stares, parents rushing their little kids to cross the street and get away from the three of you.

At first, you just thought it was a coincidence. After all, you weren't really processing things fully since the events of the day before. You didn't sleep last night. You haven't eaten since. Things were beginning to blur together. But pretty soon, you would know exactly what was going on.

As you entered the doors of the synagogue, your family went and sat in their usual spots, but what you began to notice as the service started was that those who usually sat around you had moved away—some even to the exact opposite side of the room. Your family was on an island of emptiness.

There's no way people know what happened. Please tell me people don't know, you started to think to yourself, suddenly fully awake and aware of the situation.

As the service began, your dad got up to take his place on the platform, like he did every single Sunday morning, to greet those who were in attendance.

But as he started to walk up to the front, one of the other leading teachers in the congregation, a close friend of your family, stopped him in his tracks.

"We're going to have you sit with your family today. I'm sorry," he whispered to your dad with a hand placed on your dad's chest.

"Wait what? But this is my responsibility to this church. I've done this every week for years," your dad responded.

"Not today," the man answered. "Please have a seat. We'll explain."

Dumbfounded, your dad found his way back to where you and your mom were sitting. You observed as your mom immediately

SOMETHING IS MISSING

grabbed his hand, almost as if she knew what was taking place before their very eyes.

The man who stopped your father a moment earlier took the platform and said, "Good morning church. Before we start the service here this morning, we must discuss a situation that has arisen in one of our most committed and faithful families. Not to mention that this is also a man who has been leading and teaching here for many years."

He motioned to where the three of you were sitting, and whispers began to fill the rest of the room.

Our lives are over, you think to yourself.

He continued from the platform, "As you all know, we believe in bringing situations to light that could be harmful to our congregation. There have been many concerns brought to our attention over the last couple months about this family and what has been happening with their oldest son in the community. Many of you know that these things have been extremely sinful and downright harmful to the law and teachings of God. And yesterday, it was brought to our attention that this situation has escalated to a point of no return. This young man has been charged and arrested, and we are sure he will soon be dealt with. Therefore, it is with deep sadness that I must inform you that we are asking this young man's father to step down from leadership for this season due to the shameful reality that they have been unable to lead their family in the ways of God. Thank you. Let's stand and pray together."

As if things couldn't get any worse, you now had to be a part of the family whose son murdered someone, whose father was removed from leadership in the synagogue, and whose family was asked to leave the only congregation that they've ever known. *If God wasn't mad at us before, He surely is now. Just look at what's happening*, you think to yourself.

As the man continues to pray, your mom grabs your hand and

leads you outside the doors. Your father slowly follows, almost wobbling, like his knees are going to give out.

"We need to get out of here and get home now!" your mom exclaims as she continues to pull you.

Word travels fast in this town. And even though you're unsure about God and how He feels about all of this, one thing you know for sure is if God's people, the people of the church, treated you like that, then you don't want anything to do with them for a long, long time.

As your family speed walks home, you feel as though you're gliding along, not even touching the ground, because of how deep you are in thought. The cycle of doubts, questions, and heartbreak continues to plague your mind. If either of your parents said anything to you on this walk, you simply wouldn't have heard them.

Why? Why God, why? you ask yourself over and over again.

Your parents pull ahead of you and walk hand in hand with you stumbling along slowly behind them. You find yourself looking at the ground as the questions continue to pour through your mind and overlap once more, and after several minutes of looking down, you accidentally run into the back of your dad.

"Woah, Dad, I'm so sorry. I was a little bit lost in thought I guess with everything going on, and I wasn't looking at all. I'm so sorry," you stammer.

No response. You look up at him and notice that he hasn't even moved. *Did I hurt him or something?* you ask yourself.

You follow his gaze and realize that you have made it back to your house, and your parents are standing at the very edge of the yard. As you continue to follow their unmoving eyes, you realize why they've become motionless, and you find yourself fixed in the same state.

There, on the front of the only home that your family has ever known, in bright, red letters, reads:

"MURDERER"

✠

SOMETHING IS MISSING

We will never be able to fully comprehend how mind boggling it is that no one is exempt from the forgiveness of God unless we compare it to our human standard. In the world that we live in, this would never fly. Let's think about how we deal with crimes for a moment.

There are levels of punishment depending on the level of crime that a person commits. Right? Can we all agree with this? From our earthly point of view, someone who cheats on a math test and someone who takes the life of another human being do not deserve the same punishment. One deserves a warning or potentially a zero on the test, while the other one deserves to spend the rest of their lives in jail. (I'm speaking in generalities here, so stick with me.) And this is the way that our human world has always run.

In the Old Testament, if you read through the 613 laws that the people at that time had to keep, you'll also become familiar with the fact that there were different levels of sacrifices that could be made by a person to settle the score between them and God and make things right. You didn't sacrifice your best lamb every time you messed up (this was a symbol of your best sacrifice by the way), but instead, you would burn your good crops and things of that nature. There have always been levels of punishments depending on the level of the crime in our world.

And this is why the forgiveness for sins offered by God through Jesus' sacrifice is so radically different from our way of living and thinking. In our minds, people who commit "bigger sins" deserve to spend more time asking for forgiveness, praying, reading their Bible, and so on. Whereas someone who commits a "smaller sin" should only have to pray one time or something like that.

The major problem that I have with this way of thinking is—who defines the line? Who sets the standard? Who decides when a sin is "too bad" or "not that bad"? If the lines of forgiveness are left up to us, things are going to get messy really quick, especially once you factor in that there are eight billion people and counting on earth who all have different personality types, stories, backgrounds, levels of tolerance, and so on and so forth. Do you see why God's forgiveness cannot be based on the scale of sin that we've created?

Instead of this level of forgiveness being left up to the eight billion and counting people on earth, let's leave it up to the One who created the eight billion and counting, knows them by name, and has never messed up. Sound okay to you?

Actually, we're lucky that it's left up to Him! Because here's the closing point on this section of the problem. This problem is universal. This problem of a broken, incomplete, sinful humanity is a universal issue that extends past generations, cultures, religions, personal interests, and all of the above.

This problem includes you and me.

We're living in it.

"For everyone has sinned; we all fall short of God's glorious standard" (Romans 3:23, NLT).

And: "For the wages of sin is death, but the free gift of God is eternal life through Christ Jesus our Lord" (Romans 6:23, NLT).

Sometimes, I'm really thankful that Scripture gives it to us straight. I love the way that Paul writes this verse because it doesn't exclude anyone. Everyone means everyone! We've all fallen short of the standard of perfection that God has set for us.

And if we hold this to be true, then there's no hope, right? If the Bible makes it excruciatingly clear that no matter what we've done, how good we may seem, or how Christian people think we are, we still fall short, then the game is over. The ending is written. Our fate is sealed, isn't it? Not only that, but the Bible doesn't play around with the fact that even one sin against the holy, perfect, set-apart God of the Bible condemns us to an eternity of death and Hell. All hope is lost. The story has to stop here, right?

No. Because something is missing.

What Jesus has done on the cross has taken something away, and therefore, He has given us everything.

It's time to unveil what this something is.

CLUE #4 -
EVERYONE HAS FALLEN SHORT OF GOD'S DESIRE, AND WE CANNOT MAKE THINGS RIGHT ON OUR OWN BECAUSE OUR SIN, MISTAKES, GUILT, AND SHAME STAND IN THE WAY. WE'RE ALL MURDERERS. IF NOT IN ACTIONS, WE DEFINITELY ARE IN OUR HEARTS AND MINDS. BUT JESUS HAS TAKEN SOMETHING AWAY, ERASED IT COMPLETELY, AND THIS CHANGES OUR ETERNAL DESTINY.

PART #2

THE PATH

Chapter 5

AN UNFAIR STORY OF THE COMPLETELY FAIR GOD

Welcome to "The Path." You're here! You made it! I can't believe I've kept your attention for this long, honestly. Maybe something deep inside of you is desperately waiting to uncover what this missing thing is, and you're hoping that I don't keep dragging this out to give you the answer.

Well, you're in luck. I'm not going to drag this out. I'm not one for stories, movies, or points that could be told in a smaller amount of time but instead are dragged out into much longer versions. It's painful. But I digress.

We've established the problem. Our feet have gotten wet as we've begun to see that this problem, the brokenness of humanity and what sin has done to the entire world, is universal. It doesn't just affect me. It doesn't just affect you. It doesn't just affect Christians, even! It's a universal problem that extends across every culture, language, belief, and personality. We need something or someone to step in for us.

That being said, I want to introduce you to "The Path." In our imaginary treasure hunt that is this book, we've found the treasure chest itself in the first section. And now we're looking at it. We're about to open it up and bask in its glory and beauty and wealth.

But, as all treasure hunts go, we can't experience the treasure or what's waiting inside without unlocking it. Opening it. Lifting off the cover that conceals what we've been searching for.

Therefore, we need keys. We need a device that will unlock the treasure that is so close. And that's what this section is all about: a few keys that are extremely important if we want to not only find this treasure (because we've already done that) but spend its wealth and allow it to actually impact our lives as we follow Jesus in the world that we live in.

So, let's find some keys, shall we?

In order to properly discover what is missing in this book, we have to start with the story of God. We have to figure out who He is and what He's all about if we want the payoff to be worth it. And in order to do that, we have to start at the beginning. I'm talking from the very beginning: Genesis 1.

Once upon a time.

Okay, pause: How mind-bogglingly awesome would it be if the Bible started with the phrase, "Once upon a time"?

That's not how it actually starts, but man, it would be pretty cool, wouldn't it?

How it does start is pretty epic as well. Check it out. "In the beginning God created the heavens and the earth" (Genesis 1:1, NLT).

Right off the bat, we're introduced to this amazing God who is a creator. In fact, He's the Creator. The Mastermind. The Creative Force. The Entrepreneur behind everything that we see. The first two chapters of Genesis are the story and facts behind all the things that God created, and, spoiler alert, it includes everything we see (and can't see). And there is lots of debate in the church world about whether this story of creation took place in a literal seven days or if it was much longer than that, like a couple thousand years. The theories go on, but regardless of what side you lean toward, it doesn't change the fact that the God of the Bible breathed everything we see into existence—including you.

After God has created the world and all of its inhabitants, and He breathes the first man and woman into existence, He walks alongside them. This part cannot be overlooked. This amazing, all-powerful, mighty God, since the very beginning has had a desire to walk alongside us and be in relationship with us. In fact, as I write this book, the year is 2022, and this desire of God's hasn't changed. He designed humanity to bring Him glory, to love Him, to be loved by Him, to be in relationship with Him, and to walk alongside Him. How beautiful is that?

Now, as I've said before, we get about two chapters in the Bible where things are good. We all know the story with the naked people, the Honeycrisp apple, and the dragon from Mulan's evil older brother.

This story tells us about what led to humanity's separation from intimacy with God, and our trajectory completely changes as we now have to battle against the sin that is built into our DNA and the whole of who we are. Let's pause for a moment and remind ourselves: What is sin? Most of us have a general idea of what we think it is, but I think defining sin will help us understand God better. In 1 John 3:4, we're told that sin is lawlessness, meaning that anything apart from the law (God's law, that is) is sin. And we also know that God is the standard of everything just, fair, and right. They are polar opposites. Sin and God exist on the farthest ends of the spectrum apart from each other. Anything that is of God cannot be sin, and anything that is sin cannot be of God. Onward we go.

The story of humanity is truly a tragic story—one that should make you sad if you are a believer because our close connection with God was severed from that point forward.

What follows is the truly happy and beautiful (cue the sarcastic tone) story that we love to share with children, where God decides to push the restart button and wipe the world clean with a flood—killing hundreds and thousands of people. Now, color that picture of the ark, kids! Look at those smiling giraffes! Don't forget to color in that dead body floating in the water!

Okay, sorry, had to go there. It was necessary.

The flood happens. There's a clean slate, a fresh start, a new perspective. Things are going to be better, smarter, wiser, and closer to God than ever before. Right?

Now, I want to pause here for just a minute. I don't want to take time in this chapter to sum up the story of the Bible. Why? Well, on a personal level, because I did it in my first book. But on the level of this book and its direction, I want to focus on the story of God and who He is above all else.

But the story of the flood is important to understand God's character because it's very easy to fall into the false mindset that God is evil, sadistic, and scary when we read an Old Testament story such as this one. What kind of God would do such a thing? What kind of God would allow for all of these people to die?

Now, we're beginning to understand this God's character. One of the most neglected traits of God's character is that He is just. It makes us uncomfortable and goes against what our world tells us (you know, "living my truth" and things of that nature) to believe in a God who calls the shots. He is just, fair, righteous, holy, and we cannot forget these things when we talk about the God of the Bible. He isn't a God who will allow evil, injustice, oppression, or sin to go unpunished.

I understand that it can still be overwhelming to read about this God if you're new to the idea of who He is, but I want to ask the follow up question and push a little bit farther if I may. What do you think His just nature is based on?

Is it control? Is it greed? Is it power? Why does the God of the Bible demand, seek, long, expect, and enforce justice? Well, let's read what the author has to say about how God was feeling before the flood took place.

"The Lord observed the extent of human wickedness on the earth, and he saw that everything they thought or imagined was consistently and totally evil. So the Lord was sorry he had ever made them and put them on the earth. It broke his heart" (Genesis 6:5-6, NLT).

Did you catch it? Because I sure did. In fact, as I'm typing these words, I can't look away from the phrase, "It broke his heart."

This phrase can't be moved past. If you can read that, and it doesn't gut-check you, then I don't know what will. What this Scripture does is reveal a huge characteristic of God. His heart breaks when we sin. He is led to a place of wiping the slate clean not because He was bored or just really excited about the software update for humanity 2.0 and not because He wanted to flex His power (He already breathed the entire world and universe into existence for crying out loud) but because He was heartbroken over the fact that His people—humanity—weren't living up to what He desired for them.

Well, why should they? Don't they have a say? Why should they have to follow His plans? His rules? His ideas? That sounds a bit like a dictator, doesn't it? Why should we have to follow this God? Well, you don't have to. That's why our world may be more anti-Christian than ever. We do have a choice in all of this. But maybe, just maybe, it's because God knows better than we do. It's because His desire since the beginning of time is for us to live life and live it to the full. (Some wise guy said that one time. I just can't remember who it was. Maybe Alexander Hamilton?).

Maybe this is our first key for unlocking the treasure of what is missing and that is going to allow us to live an effective, free, hope-filled, beautiful life. The key is realizing that God's desire was never to oppress, dictate, and ruin our lives. It's always been to walk alongside us, love us, even when we fall short (which is often), and release us into a true life of flourishing which can only come from what's best for us: His plans.

☩

Lost time has become a regular part of your life at this point. Ever since the news with your brother, days, weeks, even what feels like months all blend together and merge into one overwhelming yet dull existence that you find yourself living.

You and your dad finally got the paint scrubbed off the house but with a fair share of nasty comments tossed in your direction as people and families walked by. Some even stopped just to spit at you.

The synagogue isn't a place for you anymore. The only thing outside of your home is work, and if you're being completely honest, you can't believe that you even still have a job after the things that people have been saying about you and your family.

Your dad was released from his leadership position at the synagogue and is still looking for other opportunities to make money. So, needless to say, things have gotten tight.

Why is this happening to us? you often wonder to yourself over and over again. You can't help but search for the why behind this situation.

But today is an important day. Today, you will be leaving the house for something other than work, but it's not necessarily something that you're excited for.

It's court hearing day.

Today will determine the future of your brother's life and not only that, but it will hopefully clear up some of the rumors and details of what really happened with him. All that you've been told at this point is what the officers brought to your front door, that your brother had killed someone. And based on the way that he was acting the last time you two talked in your room, it all adds up.

"Time to go!" your mother yells from downstairs.

Looking in the mirror, you run your fingers through your hair one more time and then head down to meet them as they're walking out the front door.

Here we go, you think to yourself.

After the long walk to arrive at the court, you finally walk in the doors of the room where the hearing is going to take place in a few short moments. Your family is escorted to the front of the room, but you are taken aback by how many people are there. The noise is deafening as every seat is taken and people are filling the aisles. What is happening?

As your family is being escorted to the front, you pick up on what some of the people are talking about. In fact, some of the people here are trying to get the attention of the guards and officers on duty.

"No, sir, you don't understand, this is treason we're talking about! If you don't take action, a revolt is coming, and it'll be on you!" a man shouts angrily.

You hear another one say, "This trial today should be postponed until we clear that case up! You don't understand the repercussions of not dealing with this man. He's dangerous! And unpredictable!"

Before you can fully process who or what these men could even be talking about, you find yourself seated in the front row of this courtroom, and the man in charge, whom you recognize as the Roman governor, takes the stand and quiets everyone down.

"Good afternoon. My name is Pontius Pilate, and today, we're gathered to review the case of first-degree murder that was committed three weeks ago. The defendant is Barabbas and two of his friends, all of whom are on trial for this crime. Each one of them has more than enough evidence against them not only due to the crime in question, but plenty of previous crimes as well. If found guilty today, all three men will be sentenced to the highest form of punishment, crucifixion."

At the mention of that word, your throat and chest tighten up. It doesn't take a scholar to know that when that word is thrown out, there is a very serious crime that has taken place. Not only that, but there's probably some pretty good evidence, too. It was saved for the worst of the worst.

As Pilate finishes this statement, he turns to the council of men that were on the case as well, and all of them nodded in agreement. After this, he motioned to the guard behind him who then proceeded to bring out the three men and sit them up on a podium for everyone to see. Wrists chained together. Ankles chained together. Dirty. Beaten. Tired. Hungry.

One of them is your brother.

As the hearing proceeds, you can't look away from him. It is pretty obvious that he is avoiding eye contact from your whole family due to the level of shame and even fear that he is feeling in that moment.

As Pilate continued to work through the evidence and accusations from the different eyewitnesses and other things involved, it became blindingly clear that Barabbas was the one who initiated the murder—at least as far as you can tell he was the mastermind behind it all. But something else is extremely apparent, each of the men played a role in this crime. And it may not have been the only incident of this nature. All three men. Including your very own brother.

As the hearing proceeds, you can't focus on anything other than your brother's face. Occasionally, you'll catch a word or two as Pilate continues to read the evidence stacked against the three of them. You'll also occasionally hear your mom catch her breath from crying or your dad clear his throat from disappointment. But all of that fades to the background in your mind. You are focused on trying to make eye contact with him, even for just a second.

Finally, you're snapped back into reality when the room erupts

SOMETHING IS MISSING

in noise. People begin cheering and declaring that justice has prevailed once again.

"Wait what?" you almost scream to your parents.

"That's it. He's guilty. Two weeks until crucifixion day," your dad mumbles morbidly.

Your whole body goes numb. You knew that this possibility was so real, and yet you fought it off every time it reared its ugly head in your mind.

The guards grab the arms of the men and begin to lead them out of the room. Finally, you stand to your feet and yell your brother's name, so he finally looks over and makes eye contact with you.

With tears in your eyes and knees shaking so bad you aren't entirely sure how you're still standing, you muster the ability to wink, signifying to him that everything is going to be alright.

Your brother immediately bursts into tears and turns his back to walk out of the room.

The signal was not returned.

For the first time ever, the signal was not returned.

The air feels empty. Dry. Hopeless.

This is really the end.

✝

Now, one more thing I want to include about the character of God as we draw this particular chapter to a close: it's how God describes Himself. Did you know He's done this?

In the book of Exodus, God is speaking to Moses, who was the man that led the Israelites (God's people) out of slavery in Egypt after 400-something long hard years. So yeah, he's kind of a big deal.

But in this particular section of Exodus, God is speaking to Moses directly and verbally, which was something that they did often. How cool would that be? To be able to speak to God face to face. Like, I picture Moses trying to be humble about the fact that he and God spoke face to face on a somewhat regular basis. His Israelite friends are like, "Moses are you even listening? We've been trying to tell you our plan for a few minutes now!" And Moses replies, like, "Yo, I'm so sorry guys. God just sent me the funniest Tik Tok, and I am dying. Seriously, He is just the best."

Anyway.

On one of these occasions where God and Moses are talking to each other, God provides Moses (and us today) with his personal bio. His writeup. His resume. Check this out.

"Then the Lord came down in a cloud and stood there with him; and he called out his own name, Yahweh. The Lord passed in front of Moses, calling out, "Yahweh! The Lord! The God of compassion and mercy! I am slow to anger and filled with unfailing love and faithfulness. I lavish unfailing love to a thousand generations. I forgive iniquity, rebellion, and sin. But I do not excuse the guilty'" (Exodus 34:5-7a, NLT).

Are you kidding me?

This God could have described Himself any way He wanted to, here. I mean, come on, He's God. And yet, He decides to focus on a few very specific things about His character: slow to anger, compassionate, merciful, full of unfailing love, faithful.

And on top of all of those things, He shares with us that He is just. He doesn't excuse the guilty. He's fair. He's holy. Yet again, going back to the point that we made earlier, He's perfect.

This brings me to what I've been trying to put language to in these pages so far. This perfect, just, fair, loving, merciful God who cannot coexist with sin did something drastic. Something bold. Something that will rewire humanity and history forever.

In fact, this thing that He decides to do is even a little bit unfair. You and I and every human being who has walked this planet benefits from this decision that God made.

He decided to send His only Son to this world to die.

Do you want me to take this a step further and make it even more mind-boggling?

This was God's plan all along.

The decision to send His Son to die for our sins wasn't a game-time decision. It wasn't done on a whim. It wasn't just a feeling. It was premeditated redemption. This wonderful, amazing, huge God is also extremely kind and gracious, so much so that He had the story of our salvation written out for us. Paul tells us in Galatians 1:4 that "Jesus gave his life for our sins, just as God our Father planned, in order to rescue us from this evil world in which we live" (NLT). Wow. Jesus was on a mission—one that had been written up since the dawn of time—to save our souls.

Yes, He lived a perfect life. Yes, He walked this planet for thirty-three years in a human body. Yes, He performed miracles and taught sermons that challenged the world to this very day. Yes, He started a movement that took off and became Christianity. Yes, He raised up some of the most powerful thought leaders of all time to follow His example. Yes, He spoke many provocative and powerful truths that challenge the very core of our beings as humans. Yes, He provided the ultimate example for how to live and exist with God and with people and do it all faithfully.

But despite everything that He did (and I for one am immensely and indescribably thankful that He did those things), He was sent here to die. For you and for me. The broken. The lost. The sinners. Those who could never measure up to God or be good enough to meet the standards needed to enter Heaven based on our own record. Those of us with a problem that we can't escape.

Jesus was sent here to die for us.

That, my friends, is extremely unfair.

From our human point of view. From our earthly perspective. From our understanding of justice, laws, and right and wrong. It seems as though this decision makes no sense. It doesn't add up. It's entirely unfair.

And our entire beings should be thankful that this perfect, holy, set-apart, just, fair God had planned all along to save humanity in a way that seems blatantly unfair from where we're standing.

Because of what happened through the death of His Son, Jesus Christ, has allowed for something to go missing, and because of that, everything can be found.

Because of this completely fair God making a seemingly unfair decision in our favor, the blood of Jesus was shed, death was defeated, Hell was silenced, the grave was stomped on, the veil was torn, Heaven was opened wide, and the cost of our sin has gone missing.

Did you get that?

Did you catch it?

Do not turn the page or move an inch without sitting on that truth. Because that truth changes everything. That truth is the reason why I'm writing this book and the truth that could, in fact, set you free.

The weight of your sin, which should be on your shoulders, is missing.

The admission fee for Heaven, which should be up to us to pay, has been covered in full.

The payment for our lives, which should be eternal suffering and pain, is reversed.

The shackles of our struggles, which we can never unlock on our own, have been shattered by the King.

The battle against sin, which could never be won by even our strongest efforts, has been won by Him.

Jesus' body in the grave, which should've been the end of the story, was raised after three days.

Something is missing. Jesus has taken it. We are free.

KEY #1 -
GOD'S HEART HAS NEVER BEEN TO OPPRESS OR CONTROL YOU. HE'S GOD. ALL-POWERFUL. ALMIGHTY. IF HE WANTED TO CONTROL YOU, HE COULD. BUT HIS HEART FOR YOU AND FOR HUMANITY SINCE THE BEGINNING OF TIME HAS BEEN TO WALK ALONGSIDE US, LOVE US UNCONDITIONALLY, AND SHOW US THAT HIS WAYS ARE ACTUALLY THE KEY FOR US TO FIND TRUE JOY, PEACE, AND HAPPINESS.

Chapter 6

YOU'RE NOT THAT POWERFUL

I kind of revealed my hand a little bit in the past chapter, I must admit. As I wrote that final paragraph of the page before this one, I took a step back and realized, "That's it. That's the heart of this book. It's the message that's going to carry this work out into the world."

But I also must admit something else: we are far from the end of this journey together. Just because we've begun to really get into what is missing doesn't mean we're anywhere close to figuring out what that means, why it really matters, and how this should affect our lives going forward.

So, don't you worry. I'm not done with you yet. You'll still have to put up with me for a few more chapters.

For the sake of over-clarifying myself because I want to make sure it really sticks in our heads and hearts as we continue to explore this aspect of our stories together, I want to restate it one more time.

The thing missing is the cost of your sin. It's a cost, by the

SOMETHING IS MISSING

way, that you are absolutely incapable of and unable to repay on your own. It's a cost, by the way, that disqualifies and prevents you from entering the gates of Heaven or having a relationship with God. It's a cost, by the way, that each and every human being has on their shoulders.

But only until they accept what Jesus has done for them. That's the exchange. That's the turnover. That's the moment that the unbearable and unshakable cost and weight is relieved. In fact, that's the only moment that the cost and weight can be relieved. There is no other way.

There's a story in Scripture where Jesus makes a pretty bold and upfront claim about His involvement in this whole process. It's in John chapter 14, and Jesus is hanging out with His disciples when the conversation takes a turn toward what's going to happen when Jesus leaves them.

He begins to reassure them not to fear because there is more than enough room in His Father's house for them (with lots and lots of room), and not only that, but once He does leave, they know where He is going and how to get there.

Now, this leaves the disciples extremely confused. Don't even try to flex. If you put yourself in those shoes, you'd be extremely confused as well.

Personally, I like to picture this moment full of awkward silence. Jesus explains how they're all going to be with Him in His Father's house, and they have the address to throw in their Google Maps, so not to fear, and all of that good stuff, and then, I like to picture the room getting really quiet.

For like a whole minute.

You know how awkward that is. You've been there.

And then, finally, Thomas (who is so awesome by the way) breaks the silence and asks the question that everyone in the room was thinking but was too scared to ask for themselves: "'No, we don't know, Lord,' Thomas said. 'We have no idea where you are going, so how can we know the way?" (John 14:5). Man, I love this. Thomas just calls it like it is and is brutally honest that they have no idea what Jesus is talking about.

And this is where it gets spicy. The way that Jesus responds is so powerful, and it's so important for us today. What He does in one sentence is prove that no amount of good deeds, no amount of nice personality, no other religion, no religious practice, no striving for perfection, nothing else can get us to Heaven but Him. Look at this.

"Jesus told him, 'I am the way, the truth, and the life. No one can come to the Father except through me'" (John 14:6, NLT).

Are you getting this?!

There is no other way to Heaven but Jesus. There is no other way to freedom than Jesus. There is no better relationship than with Jesus. He is the ultimate source of all of these things and every single thing that our hearts have thirsted for. They're all found in our Savior. The exclusivity of Jesus cannot be missed.

This is a game-changing idea.

You see, there's a realization we have to come to here, and I think the ramifications echo and ripple through multiple different stages of life, cultures, and experiences of those who may be reading this.

That realization is the fact that if there was any other way to get into Heaven and experience true intimacy with God while on earth other than Jesus' sacrifice, then Jesus' death would have been pointless. If there was literally any other option for us as human beings to achieve what Jesus did without Him going through what He went through, then God is cruel, and the gospel story is a bit of a tragic and confusing and pointless story.

Imagine if we could experience salvation on our own. Imagine that Jesus dies this horrible, painful, bloody, lonely, undeserved death, and a few days later, His disciples are like, "Yo, that was some wild stuff. Tensions are really high, and the government officials want us dead, so it's good that we've memorized enough Scripture and haven't listened to too much explicit music so that we can get to Heaven when we die. At least, I hope we've done enough."

No! No, no, no. A million times no. If there were a way to achieve Heaven on our own, I think we'd get in too many fights establishing what the line is between good enough and not good enough to ever make any progress. We should be thankful for the fact that the line that determines if we are saved or not isn't based on us or anything that we could create as people. It's based on God alone!

There is no other way to get to Heaven or enter into a relationship with the Creator of the universe. The only doorway into those experiences is through the person, example, and, most importantly, the death and resurrection of Jesus Christ. Accepting and believing in what He did, that He paid the final cost and price for our sins and mistakes, is the only way to escape the universal problem of sin and step into the beautiful rescue mission of salvation.

Jesus' sacrifice wasn't in vain. He didn't give up His life to add just another solution to this universal problem of sin. He did it to become the end-all and be-all solution for the universal problem of sin: no matter how big or how small or how hidden or how obvious the sin may be. Jesus came to be the One to carry the weight, pay the price, and shed His blood for sin so that you and I never have to. Remember, the Bible makes it undeniably clear that we are sinners through and through. On our own, we cannot change our sinful nature.

Have you ever wondered why Jesus' last words on the cross were, "It is finished"?

It's because He was rewriting the story, and this process of striving, earning, and playing the part of perfection was over for us. Does this mean we can do whatever we want now? Well, no, and we'll get to that later; but it does mean that, instead of striving to be good enough and attempting to measure up, we can accept the fact that Jesus was already more than good enough, and His death equals our life.

You're not that powerful.

Here I go hurting feelings again. Taking shots at egos. But it's the truth. You're not. And you were never designed to be.

For me personally, I'm so thankful that I'm no longer powerful enough to be good enough. I submitted that power to Jesus when I gave my life to Him and allowed His blood to cover everything I've done, everything I am doing, and everything I will do.

I see a fork in the road as I'm attempting to describe this decision. And both paths have a lot to do with power and control, but it all comes down to who holds dominion over our lives and hearts.

You could walk one road. Scripture tells us this is a wide road (meaning lots of people walk down it). Look at what Jesus has to say about it. "'You can enter God's Kingdom only through the narrow gate. The highway to Hell is broad, and its gate is wide for the many who choose that way" (Matthew 7:13, NLT). Did you know the highway to Hell was biblical? AC/DC had it figured out, I guess. But on this wide road is where you decide to keep the power in your hands. Whether that means you reject God completely or you are kind of halfway in, halfway out on this whole Jesus thing. And if this is the path you choose to walk, you hold a lot of power because, when you fall short, mess up, sin, stumble, whatever you want to call it, let's be honest, the consequences and weight of those things all fall on you.

It's funny because choosing the path of living for yourself doesn't actually hold that much power. It may give the illusion of power. But in reality, you hold no control at all. Control holds you. When we choose to live for ourselves and hang on to our own lives, sin owns us. We aren't free at all, but we're slaves to the exact thing that God opposes.

Don't worry, though. There's another road to walk down. The Bible likes to describe this one as narrow. "But the gateway to life is very narrow and the road is difficult, and only a few ever find it" (Matthew 7:14, NLT). On this path, you give everything you

SOMETHING IS MISSING

have to God. You give Him the keys and the control and decide to follow Him every day. You believe that Jesus died for you, and not only was His body killed on the cross, but the cost of your sins was, too. And now the power is in His hands. You stay faithful to Him and give Him all that you have.

So, which path is your life leading you down?

For some of you, this is harder to answer than it is for others. For some of you, just reading this paragraph makes you realize that you're on the wrong path. You like having the power in your hands. Hopefully, I can continue to convey the fact that that's not where the power belongs, and not only that, but you're better off not holding it at all.

But for some of you, this question of the path is much harder because you think you're on the right path. Even reading this, you're telling yourself that you are. You go to church. Maybe you even tithe. You call yourself a Christian. But you don't share your faith with people. You don't love people of all races and backgrounds and stories in your heart and mind. You gossip. You're selfish. You live for yourself. You're living a lukewarm life, and you may not actually be on the narrow path of Jesus' way. Read Revelation 3:15-20 if you have a second. Ouch.

The path that your heart is walking down determines your life now and for eternity. Stop trying to hold the power and walk the path where everything is based on your actions and decisions. Hand it to Jesus. I promise He's powerful enough to carry it, and I also promise that He already paid for it on the cross.

Give the control to Him.

You're not that powerful, so stop pretending to be.

☦

"I'm so scared," your brother mutters from the other side of the table after what feels like forever of your whole family sobbing and being unable to string together words.

It's crucifixion eve.

How did it arrive so fast?

The officials have allowed for a final visit between the inmates and family members before the destruction planned for tomorrow takes place.

"Son, I'm sorry that all of this is happening. I wish we were able to be with you more through the whole process. You must be so scared," your dad says shakily from his side of the table.

"No Dad. This isn't your place to apologize. I've been ignoring the warnings from everyone around me and running with a crowd that I never should've been with in the first place. I never thought I'd end up here on death row, but my decisions have brought me here. I'm just as responsible for what happened that night. If you only knew about all the other times too. It was just a matter of time until I was caught. Believe me, I'm guilty," your brother says somewhat confidently, but you can hear the fear underlying every word.

Your mom begins to speak up but quiets herself again. Maybe she's unsure of what to say in a moment like this. Maybe she's unsure of how to say it.

"Five minutes!" the guard yells from where he's posted at the door to the room.

"Well, I guess we better wrap this up," your brother says, tears beginning to fill his eyes once more.

You've never seen him like this—fear showing in his every breath and movement. He's gripped by emotion because of the devastation that he knows is waiting right on the other side of him going to sleep tonight. As far as you can remember, he has always been strong, put together, somewhat even unemotional because of how confident he comes off. It's almost sickening to see him this way.

But you'll take seeing him this way over never seeing him again.

"So, is there anything that we need to know about tomorrow?

We don't want you to feel alone for one second," your father says, reaching across the table to grab your brother's hand, but he pulls it back slightly.

"Trust me, I've felt alone for years. If I have to feel alone tomorrow, it won't be anything new. Maybe it'll just be the last time I have to feel that way," your brother says angrily through the tears dripping down his face.

"I see," your father says, fighting back anger in his voice. "Well, I have to say this won't be the last time you feel lonely. After what you've done, you're going to spend eternity separated from Go—"

"Hey! That's enough!" your mom screams.

I cannot believe this is how the last time we will ever be together as a family is going, you think to yourself in disgust.

"That's time. Back to your cell," the guard says as he escorts your brother out of the room.

The three of you left at the table sit there for a minute to compose yourselves, dry your tears, and gather your things. After a minute or two, you get up and begin to walk out of the room.

The guard who was in the room the entire time stops the three of you as you're walking out and says, "Since he wouldn't give you any information about tomorrow, I will. It's not often that crucifixion criminals have families that want to be there for them. Get here at dawn. We will begin the walk from here and finish it when we reach Golgotha. We usually have a little ceremony and reviewing of the cases here with the governor of Rome before we begin the walk."

Your parents both nod their heads, and your dad mutters, "Thank you, sir."

As your family walks out of the cell and begins the journey back home, it feels like a death sentence has been put on all of you. It's been months since the officers arrived at your door with the news, yet it also feels like yesterday. Ever since that moment, your family knew that things would change forever, and it's hard to believe that in less than twenty-four hours, he'll be dead.

Hopeless. Angry. Broken. Confused. These are the feelings that rush through your heart and mind, all at the same time.

As the walk continues, so do your thoughts. Deeper and deeper they get the farther that you get from where your brother is being held.

Before all this, we went to church, that is, when the church accepted people like us, you think to yourself. *Before all this, my dad had a job. He was one of the most respected leaders in our town. Now, all of that is gone. Before all this, I had a brother. My best friend. Someone to look up to. Do I even believe in God anymore?* you ask yourself. *Why would I believe in a God who would allow such terrible things to happen to my family? That's not a God that I want to serve. That's not a God I want to submit to. Maybe it's good that this has happened. Maybe it's good that we're no longer a part of the faith community. Maybe I never even wanted it in the first place. Maybe I never would have been a believer if my parents hadn't raised me this way.*

The thoughts and questions continue to flood your mind as you walk. You're not entirely sure how to make them stop or even if you should make them stop.

But what you do know, without a doubt, is a newfound bitterness and anger has formed in your heart. And that's the only thing in this moment that is certain.

☦

I'll never forget the day I wrote this phrase in my notes, "We don't have to achieve Heaven. We can receive it."

That'll preach, I thought to myself.

I was preparing an Easter message for the group of students that I lead and preach to on a weekly basis, and we were asking the question, "What is the point of Easter?" For the month following the holiday that is so famous to the Christian church, we were diving deep in order to figure out the why behind it all.

The reason we decided to do a series not leading up to Easter but following and reflecting on it was because I didn't want the season to go by without truly understanding why it matters so much. In fact, I've heard some pastors and Bible scholars say that without the Easter story, our faith and the stock we put in Jesus wouldn't be as solid. In fact, it wouldn't hold up much at all.

Not many people would argue with the claim that Jesus was an amazing teacher and leader and historical figure who was murdered for His faith, but without the Easter story, that's just about all He is. Just a good teacher. Just a leader. Just a man. Maybe a dose of unstableness in there.

But we know as Christians that the story doesn't end there. We know that He rose again after three days, and His body had fresh oxygen in His lungs and blood pumping through His veins. By doing so, He defeated death, Hell, and the grave for anyone and everyone who believed in Him.

We know the story. People who don't go to church or believe in God know the story. But do we realize how much that story changed for the world? How the history of humanity and pathway to God and process for salvation all changed because of that story?

As I was preparing that specific message for those students, this thought hit me. In the Old Testament, before Jesus did what He did when He canceled our debt, we had to achieve our way to Heaven. This means that, time and time again, we failed to please God. At the time, the sacrificial system was in place, and whenever a sin was committed, the accuser had to sacrifice a crop or an animal to God to pay for their sins. The cost was on our shoulders. We had to figure it out.

But because of Jesus, because of His sacrifice, because He declared that it is finished, because the weight of our sin and the price that we were supposed to pay is now missing and completely written out of the record, we no longer have to achieve Heaven. We can receive it.

It's a gift (Ephesians 2:8) with no receipt. It's been paid for in full, and we aren't powerful enough to give it back or buy it on our own. Instead, it's waiting at the doorstep of our hearts for each and every one of us. All we have to do is accept it. All we have to do is realize and accept the fact that Jesus has allowed the most beneficial something to go missing forever, and He has no intention of bringing it back or using it against us.

Have you ever had that friend (it may be a stretch calling them a friend) who expects every single little thing to be paid back? Don't get me wrong. I know what it's like to live on a tight budget and make sure things get paid back. But I'm talking about the people who you borrow clothing from or something like that, and they're like, "I don't even wear that anymore. You can have it." And you respond, "Oh, no way! I really like it. Thanks so much." To which they respond, "Yeah no problem! I paid $20 for it, so how's $10 sound?" Right...

It's one thing if you offer to buy something off of them, or they need the money to get a new version—that's all fine. But it's safe to assume we've all had friends like this at some point. Every fry you share, every cent of the ticket they bought you, everything is expected to be paid back in full.

Jesus doesn't operate like that. In fact, He takes the price tag that you could never afford, pays for it, and assures you that it's a gift. Now that's a good God.

This gift is yours. Take it! Right now. Put this book down and invite God into your heart by recognizing your need for Jesus and believing in what He did on the cross if you haven't before. The Bible tells us, "If you openly declare that Jesus is Lord and believe in your heart that God raised him from the dead, you will be saved" (Romans 10:9, NLT). Seriously! The cost of your sin is gone because of Jesus. If you believe in who He is, He can save you in a moment. He's that powerful. His sacrifice means that much.

It doesn't matter if you're at home, at work, at school, outside, on the couch, on the toilet, or anywhere in between. Believe in Him, and you'll be saved. Don't worry. This book will be here waiting when you get back.

And if you're someone who has accepted the gift already, take a moment to reflect on the cross. On the sacrifice. On the gift. Remind yourself how you've been set free because your chains have gone missing, and you no longer have to hold the power of carrying them around anymore.

Stop trying to measure up. (Sounds familiar, doesn't it?) Stop striving. Stop trying to prove yourself. You're not that powerful. But Jesus is, and the battle is already won. Past tense. Joy, freedom, and peace are not past tense. Those are available right now in the present, and they won't run out in the future if the source of them is Jesus.

KEY #2 -
THE ONLY WAY TO EXPERIENCE ETERNAL LIFE IN HEAVEN AND FULL LIFE ON EARTH IS THROUGH JESUS AND WHAT HE DID ON THE CROSS. WE ARE NOT POWERFUL ENOUGH TO EARN OUR WAY TO HEAVEN OR QUALIFIED ON OUR OWN, BUT BECAUSE OF WHAT'S MISSING, WE HAVE BEEN MADE ENOUGH THROUGH THE ONE WHO HAS ALWAYS BEEN MORE THAN ENOUGH

Chapter 7

THE SCALE IS BROKEN

I have to admit I love when people take the time to ask about where a book idea came from or what the process was like for me to write it. With my first book, *Love More Worry Less,* I wasn't expecting this question, and as I started to get asked it throughout the weeks and months after the book's release, it became one of my favorite things to respond to (except for when people asked if it was a school project. No seriously, I was asked this). Why has this become one of my favorite questions?

Well, writing a book is hard work. Like, sometimes it can be brutal, to be honest. Sometimes, you don't feel like sitting down to write, but you do so in order to get into the habit and discipline of doing so. (This is true for many things in life.) On the other hand, sometimes you sit down to write, and it's like someone else is doing it for you. The words just fly onto the page, and it's clear that inspiration has struck from somewhere. Those times are extremely fun. But on top of all that, not only is it hard work, it's extremely vulnerable. As I sat down and started to write this book, I asked a few people in my life to read each section as it was finished. One of my friends stated, after reading the first section, "The process of writing something like this has to be extremely vulnerable, doesn't it?"

Yes. He was spot on. The process of taking concepts and ideas that are laid on one's heart and communicating them on the page is no easy task. It's a constant battle of knowing what will land and what won't—trying to write in a way that people from all walks and circles of life can understand. It's not always fun. But man, I love it.

"So, why did I write this book?" you ask.

Well, thanks so much for asking! How'd you know that's one of my favorite questions of all time to be asked?

It's rather simple. I felt led to write this particular book because, if we don't live like these concepts and ideas are true, we are robbing Jesus of His sacrifice, God of His glory, life of its potential, and Heaven of its wonder.

What we're talking about, this idea of the cross shifting everything and the cost of our sin going missing, is nothing short of paradigm-shifting and game-changing. This is the jump-off point for anyone following Jesus for the first time and the anchor that keeps those who have been following Jesus for a lifetime pursuing the King every day and experiencing life in new ways.

Something is missing. That's a big deal. That's why this book is out in the wild. It's so that you, too, can realize and appreciate what is missing and let it change your life. Maybe even let it change the lives of those you love.

☦

As you walk into the courtroom this morning, the crowd is at an unbelievable level of excitement.

You begin having Deja vu to the court hearing a few weeks

back, when people were attempting to get the attention of the guards and were warning them about some "dangerous man," but this level of energy in the crowd is a hundred times more. As you follow the guard who pushes and moves people out of your family's way, you catch all kinds of statements from random people.

"Can you believe they finally got him?"

"Do you think he's guilty?"

"They don't even have room for him for today's crucifixion."

"I was in the crowd that was with him a few days ago. Unbelievable stuff. He's awesome!"

The three of you reach the marked-off section for family members in the front of the room, and you take your seats. You notice that your parents both have begun to notice the weird energy and things happening in the room.

You've never been to a crucifixion before, but it doesn't take past experience to know that they probably don't happen like this. Something is going on.

Finally, Pontius Pilate takes the stage at the front of the room and addresses the crowd, announcing that the crucifixion execution is going to begin. As he continues talking and going over the details of the case, he is suddenly interrupted by a group of men that make up a council of officials and leaders.

They barge onto the stage and throw a man down at the feet of Pilate. The entire room goes silent.

What in the world is going on? you think to yourself. *Who is this man laying at the feet of the governor?*

One of the council members speaks up and says, "This man has been leading our people astray by telling them not to pay their taxes to the Roman government and by claiming he is the Messiah, a king" (Luke 23:2, NLT).

A claim of treason. In the middle of a case about murder. What is this?

Pilate bends down to look at this man on the ground in the

face, and he asks him rather quietly, "Are you the king of the Jews?" (Luke 23:3, NLT).

After a couple seconds of complete silence, the man responds, "You have said it" (Luke 23:3, NLT).

As soon as the words are uttered, the entire room erupts. The crowd of people behind your family is screaming terrible things about this man who has been brought before Pilate. Accusations of Him being Satan, a liar, a thief, blasphemous, and combinations of words you didn't even know existed.

This man is really hated, you think to yourself.

Pilate brings the man to his feet and dusts him off. The crowd continues to scream and roar as loud as possible. From where you are standing, the look on Pilate's face is nothing but confusion.

Pilate turns to the leading priests and to the crowd and says, "I find nothing wrong with this man!" (Luke 23:4, NLT).

Then they become insistent. "But he is causing riots by his teaching wherever he goes—all over Judea, from Galilee to Jerusalem!" (Luke 23:5, NLT).

Pilate then calls in King Herod to check the facts and details of the accusations of this man. And after a long time of checking with priests, leaders, and rulers, along with the crowd continuing to roar with accusations and claims, Pilate finally returns with a decision.

"You brought this man to me, accusing him of leading a revolt. I have examined him thoroughly on this point in your presence and find him innocent. Herod came to the same conclusion and sent him back to us. Nothing this man has done calls for the death penalty. So I will have him flogged, and then I will release him," Pilate said (Luke 23:14-16, NLT).

When Pilate said this, potentially the loudest roar of the morning arose from the crowd. People demanded that Pilate change his mind and have this man killed. The accusations and mocking continued all around where your family was sitting.

And then, a chant arose from the crowd. It started slowly, but after a minute or two, everyone seemed to have joined in. They were chanting, "Release Barabbas! Release Barabbas!"

Even though he was the one who got your brother in so much trouble, so your family knew his name well, it became very clear that his reputation was known around town. People knew that he was being crucified today for murder, and yet, they preferred him being released over this man on the stage with Pilate.

Another chant rose up from the crowd, and this one was even louder than the first one: "Crucify him! Crucify him!"

For the third time, Pilate demanded, "Why? What crime has he committed? I have found no reason to sentence him to death. So I will have him flogged, and then I will release him" (Luke 23:22, NLT).

But the crowd got even louder still, toeing the line of getting violent if their decision was not honored. The look on Pilate's face was still one of confusion, but it was now mixed with a dose of fear.

Finally, he gave in. He declared that this man, apparently his name was Jesus, was going to be crucified today due to the people's decision. He also honored their other decision and released Barabbas to them.

"This cannot be happening!" your father suddenly shouts from where he's sitting.

The man who was the mastermind behind your brother being caught was being let go without a second thought. This wasn't fair. This didn't make any sense. What just happened?

The crowd cheers and celebrates this new decision that was made in front of them. The three criminals are led out in front of the crowd. Each of them is given a cross, their own cross, to carry toward Golgotha.

The death march had begun. Your brother, his friend, and this new Jesus character. The end was here.

✟

SOMETHING IS MISSING

The conversation around diet, exercise, and weight has always made me uncomfortable. Not because I dislike any of these things—in fact, it's the opposite. I'm all for these things and the immense benefits that come from them.

The reason why I'm uncomfortable with these kinds of things is because I've always struggled with gaining weight.

Yes, you read that right—gaining weight.

Now, in junior high and early high school, this wasn't a big deal. I was young. I was a soccer player. It was totally fine that I wasn't super muscular or strong. But as I got to the end of my time in high school and even early college years, I started to get serious about working out and dieting.

And before we go any further, I know some of you are thinking, "Wow, I'd do anything to have the problem of not being able to put weight on." And you might be right. This may be a problem that isn't even worth talking about. But I have to say that being called "skin and bones," "skeleton," "tiny," and things of that nature aren't fun either. Paired with the constant attempt to stuff myself, count my calories, and lift multiple times a week, there was a lot of frustration and anger in terms of how I felt about my body for a few years.

I remember one summer in particular, right after I graduated high school, I told myself that I was done messing around, and it was time to look like Dwayne "The Rock" Johnson. Okay, maybe that's a stretch. My more realistic goal was to look like Tom Holland's Spider-Man, because who wouldn't want to look like him. Just an all around stud.

So I worked hard. I'm talking four to five days a week. I was in the gym, lifting weights and training my body. After every workout, I was drinking protein shakes, and every morning for breakfast, I had a protein bar. I ate so much chicken that I didn't even know what to do with myself, and I was convinced that this was going to be when the tides changed with my body. At the start of this intense summer workout program, I believe I weighed 146.

I was all in. I stuck to this plan for months, only taking a few off days here and there. And on the surface, I was beginning to look like I was working out hard, which is a fantastic feeling. So I assumed that my body weight had to be following suit and most likely in dramatic ways.

As that summer came to an end, and protein powder was beginning to drip out of my nose at that point, I finally decided to weigh myself. I had weighed myself at the beginning of this journey so that I'd have some gauge of where I started, but I tried to hold off for a few months of using a scale so that the payoff would be extra rewarding.

But the time was finally here. Game time. So much time, energy, and effort were put into these last couple months. I was eager and excited as I stepped on to the scale. I remember barely even being able to look at the numbers at first because I was too exhilarated to see what my new weight was—what my effort had led to.

Finally, I peeked through squinted eyes down at the scale to see my new and improved weight.

149.

You have got to be kidding me.

All of that for three pounds?!

I worked hard. I felt like I did (almost) everything right. My overall strength improved so much. I ate too much. This isn't fair.

The scale must be broken, I thought to myself.

So, I did what any human being does in a moment like that. I stepped off, took a breath, and stepped back on.

149.

Okay, I need a new scale, I laughed to myself. So I stepped off and even gave it an extra second this time. I allowed it to recalibrate and stepped back on once more.

149.

Ouch.

Now, I'm not here to try to get you to pity me or feel bad for the fact that putting on muscle and gaining strength has always been a problem for me. Believe me, I know there are much worse hands to be dealt in life in terms of body struggles. And I've gotten to the point of accepting my body type and knowing that naturally I'll get to where I need to be if I keep putting in the work. Plus, not being able to gain weight means I can eat just about whatever I want. So I'll just take advantage of that for now, thank you very much.

I love the moments in Scripture that point us to a similar conclusion. "The scale must be broken." In fact, I think that realizing and seeing some of the moments where our perfectly just God allowed the scale to be broken in our favor is one of the most beautiful and freeing aspects of the Bible that we can look to and pull from. Because, if you believe in Jesus, the scale is actually broken in your favor. Not only is it broken in your favor, but it's so beyond repair that nothing can bring it back to measuring things correctly. And this is undeniably a reason to celebrate. Let me explain.

Maybe you've picked it up already, but the fictional story that we've put ourselves into for the duration of this book isn't completely fictional. Yes, the storyline, characters, and our role in it are all made up in order for us to feel the weight of it a little bit more, but the big moments are actually factual. They're historical. This is the story of the criminal on the cross in Luke 23.

I know we are chipping away at it piece by piece in our fictional take on this story, but I wanted to include it in this chapter as well. Even if you're someone who knows this story and has heard it many times before, please read it. Don't skip over it. Meditate and feel the weight of these words. Visualize it. It's going to help this chapter have more of the impact that it needs to.

> "As they led Jesus away, a man named Simon, who was from Cyrene, happened to be coming in from

the countryside. The soldiers seized him and put the cross on him and made him carry it behind Jesus. A large crowd trailed behind, including many grief-stricken women. But Jesus turned and said to them, 'Daughters of Jerusalem, don't weep for me, but weep for yourselves and for your children. For the days are coming when they will say, "Fortunate indeed are the women who are childless, the wombs that have not borne a child and the breasts that have never nursed." People will beg the mountains, "Fall on us," and plead with the hills, "Bury us." For if these things are done when the tree is green, what will happen when it is dry?'

"Two others, both criminals, were led out to be executed with him. When they came to a place called The Skull, they nailed him to the cross. And the criminals were also crucified—one on his right and one on his left.

"Jesus said, 'Father, forgive them, for they don't know what they are doing.' And the soldiers gambled for his clothes by throwing dice.

"The crowd watched and the leaders scoffed. 'He saved others,' they said, 'let him save himself if he is really God's Messiah, the Chosen One.' The soldiers mocked him, too, by offering him a drink of sour wine. They called out to him, 'If you are the King of the Jews, save yourself!' A sign was fastened above him with these words: 'This is the King of the Jews.'

"One of the criminals hanging beside him scoffed, 'So you're the Messiah, are you? Prove it by saving yourself—and us, too, while you're at it!'

"But the other criminal protested, 'Don't you fear God even when you have been sentenced to die? We deserve to die for our crimes, but this man hasn't done anything wrong.' Then he said, 'Jesus, remember me when you come into your Kingdom.'

"And Jesus replied, 'I assure you, today you will be with me in paradise'" (Luke 23:26-43, NLT).

This is game-changing. This is the story of Jesus that burdened my heart so badly that I sat down and wrote this book about it because I couldn't get it out of my head. This story, in and of itself, (though there are countless others, too) proves that something is missing, and it's the best news we could ever receive. It is news so important that our whole lives should be structured around it.

In this story in Luke 23, we see the rules of the game changed. Throughout His life, Jesus was proclaiming and teaching about the fact that the rules and regulations were changing, but here in this story, moments before His death, He is actually exemplifying how different those rules are—how beautifully unfair those rules are.

Not to mention that speaking from the cross was excruciating. There's a reason why Jesus only utters seven statements during His time hanging there. It wasn't because He had run out of things to say, but rather, it was because when someone is crucified, even breathing becomes a nearly impossible task. In fact, the cause of death for those who were crucified wasn't the nails. It wasn't the bloodshed. It wasn't even pain in general (although that added to it, I'm sure). It was suffocation.

And in the middle of suffocating, Jesus paints the picture of redemption, of Heaven, of this broken scale. Having to pull Himself up by His feet and arms, both of which were pierced by huge barbaric nails, He declares that Heaven shouldn't feel out of reach for anyone.

Not even someone whose life is broken beyond repair. Jesus died for those stories, too. God designed the beautiful people behind those stories, too. There's a murderer in each of us. As humans, we naturally lean toward evil and sin—a stain that has marked humanity since Genesis 3.

But Jesus didn't die in vain. Jesus died so that we don't have to strive anymore. Jesus died because we will never be good enough. Jesus died because there is a standard of perfection in relation to the holy and perfect God of the Bible that you and I will never be able to reach.

Have you ever heard the phrase, "Covered by the blood of Jesus"? Does this weird anyone else out? Because, me too. I've grown up going to church and being surrounded by Christian language, but this phrase always felt weird to me. I want to take a stab at this phrase for a moment because it's actually pretty vital to understanding why this message really matters.

It helps if we look at the end of Jesus' life as a trial case, which is essentially what the story of Jesus' crucifixion and death really are when boiled down. Jesus was arrested for treason (at least in the eyes of the Pharisees). He stood before Pilate and the crowds as they decided what to do with Him (essentially His court hearing). And due to the people's anger, He was sentenced to death by crucifixion (a punishment saved for the worst of the worst). Then, Jesus died a painful, bloody, suffocating death on the cross. And we know that the moments after His death were a little bit chaotic, but we'll get to that more in the closing chapters of this book, so let's stay focused on this process of Jesus being sentenced to death.

In our modern world, when someone is arrested, hopefully for a crime they actually committed, they are taken to court where they must sit in front of a judge and jury. All of the evidence, facts, eyewitness accounts, and whatnot are read and deciphered to figure out if this person should go to jail and for how long. Once this process is done, the person is either sent away or put in prison. I know this is a very simplified version of this process, but stick with me here, okay?

Let's say the person is convicted. The evidence against them is just too much to ignore. The decision is then made of how long that person should spend in prison: anywhere from a few months to multiple lifetimes (which makes no sense to me). In some states, depending on the severity of the crime, there is a potential that the death penalty will be called for (which is something that should really make you sick as a Christ-follower, but I won't get into this now).

With all of this, what it comes down to is a matter of whether the evidence is stacked for or against the person in question. It is my prayer that, in our world, evidence should be the only thing that convicts someone to such a thing as prison—not skin color or any other prejudices that may come into play. But as we all know, this isn't always the case, either.

But here's the reason why I wanted to break all of this down. According to the standards of what decides if a person is guilty of a crime or not, in modern-day America or back in Jesus' time, it almost always has been based on evidence. It is all about weighing the two different sides of guilty and not guilty and finding out which side of the scale has more weight.

Even in Jesus' case, the officials were trying to weigh the two sides and decide if this man really was as guilty and worthy of death as the people were claiming. But the problem is that there was no evidence against Jesus. It was just some angry people who were louder and more in Pilate's face with their opinions. In fact, I highly suggest you check out the story of this trial in the gospels. What you're going to find is Pilate (the man in charge of running Jesus' sentencing like a judge) was actually rather confused about why Jesus was in this position at all. He even refutes and questions the people pushing so hard for His death, but ultimately, he gives in to what the majority wants. Seriously, check out Luke 23:1-25. It's fascinating and heartbreaking all at once.

There was no real evidence against Jesus. He was perfect and blameless, and yet He is convicted and treated as one of the worst criminals of that time. What makes this even wilder is the fact all of this lines up with Old Testament prophecies written thousands of years before. It's almost like it all went according to plan.

Here's where it gets tricky.

You and I have all of the evidence stacked against us in our case. This is the reason why we started this journey together with a section titled, "The Problem." We have a problem. Better yet, we are the problem. And this universal, humanity-sized problem is called sin. And according to the Bible, it and it alone affects and simultaneously disqualifies all of us from entering Heaven. (Read Romans 3:23, Romans 6:23, 1 John 1:8-10, or James 4:17 if you're still not convinced that you're a sinner, and not only that, but you were BORN a sinner. Spend a few moments with a toddler, and you will suddenly see the need for salvation.) We do, in fact, deserve the death penalty, according to Scripture and its view of sin.

Based on our lives alone, the scale is tipped so far toward guilt. It gets worse because, not only is it way heavier on the guilty side, but we can't make it any lighter! You and I are Barrabas. Let that sink in. We are the guilty criminal who has had their spot taken by Jesus on the cross. Woah.

This is where we circle back to that phrase, "Covered by the blood of Jesus," or even, "Washed by the blood of Jesus." I'm a very imaginative person, but that paints a pretty disturbing picture in my head. So, what does this mean?

SOMETHING IS MISSING

When I began to switch my perspective to looking at the blood of Jesus differently, it finally clicked. So I want you to think about it like this.

When you die (which you will, sorry to be that guy and spoil the ending), you're going to stand before God—the one and only God, the Creator of the universe and Designer of humanity and Architect of the world and Author of life. Yeah, that one. You're going to stand before Him as your shortcomings are read out loud. (Anyone else shaking in their boots a little bit? Like, okay, is He even going to read *that* one? Yeah, even that one.)

It sounds a little bit like a trial, doesn't it? We will stand before God as the evidence of our life is read and put on the scale (Matthew 12:36, Revelation 20:11-15).

And so, that alone will yet again solidify the fact that we're guilty. In the presence of God, we do not measure up, and in fact, we never could.

But here's where this blood thing comes in.

The blood that Jesus shed was a sacrifice in your place. Not just any sacrifice, but because He's God's perfect Son and walked this earth without sin, it's a perfect sacrifice. It's good enough to cover anything you and I could ever do. And throughout the Bible, a symbolic way that sacrifices were confirmed and made real was by the shedding of blood. Jesus definitely shed some blood. (Anyone seen *Passion of the Christ* lately? There's a reason why it's rated R. There's a whole lot of blood being shed.)

So here's where it gets good.

If you decide to follow and believe in Jesus while on earth, in this moment when God is reading your sins and shortcomings and the evidence stacked against you is getting higher and higher, He's also going to see the perfect sacrifice of Jesus that has marked your life. He's also going to see the blood that Jesus poured out for you and the fact that you received that gift that was bought for you on the cross. He's going to see that you are living in freedom because something went missing.

And the gates of Heaven will be opened to you.

Not because of you. Not because the evidence was in your favor. But actually because the evidence was not. You accepted the fact that on your own, you'd never be good enough, yet with Jesus, He makes you more than enough.

The scale is broken. Broken in your favor! In your trial, the evidence that was stacked against you (and there was plenty of it) has gone missing. You are now covered in the blood of Jesus, which means His perfect sacrifice, His death in your place, has picked up the bill that you could never pay.

If that truth doesn't put fire in your veins, then I don't know what else will.

KEY #3 -
THE EVIDENCE IN YOUR CASE IS STACKED AGAINST YOU, BUT IT HAS GONE MISSING. AND IF IT WERE THERE, YOU'D BE CONVICTED TO A LIFE SENTENCE OF SEPARATION AND SUFFERING. BUT IF YOU BELIEVE IN JESUS AND WHAT HE'S DONE, THE SCALE IS BROKEN IN YOUR FAVOR. THIS IS WHERE FREEDOM IS FOUND.

Chapter 8

THE MISSING PIECE THAT SOMEHOW MAKES US WHOLE

I've always hated just being a number.

Maybe that's a character flaw that I need to work out in my own life, but no matter what I say or do, I can't shake it. I've always hated being in settings and situations where I just fade into the background and become just another person.

In fact, people, places, and events that are geared toward making me feel like just a number often push me away. They definitely don't make the list of my favorite people to hang around or things to spend my time doing. Whether it be the outfit that I'm wearing, the latest show that I'm into, or a book that I'm reading, I like to have a unique take on it or stand out in some way. This may sound a bit self-centered, but stick with me here. There's a point I'm trying to make.

I feel like I haven't always been this way. There was a time when I fought tooth and nail to fit in with everyone around me and make sure that everything I did and said met their standards so that people would like me, and I'd fit in. Do any of my fellow people-pleasers out there relate to this struggle? People-pleasing is a form of idolatry, people, and it's no joke.

But that's a point for another time. Let's not dive too deep down that rabbit hole.

Once I found my identity in Jesus and who He truly was, I in turn discovered who I really was. I no longer needed or sought after the opinions of others, and I began to walk in the freedom and peace that comes from truly knowing the Savior and what He's done for us (allowing something to go missing). My social anxiety was alleviated. My desire to please everyone was knocked down a few pegs. And I found myself set free from the weight of other people's opinions. I think Jesus wants this for all of us.

On a very personal level, once I made this switch, I no longer wanted to be just another number or a face in the crowd. I wanted to be different, to swim upstream—in small ways and also in ways that mattered. It was as if understanding Jesus unlocked a part of my personality that I didn't know was there.

I gotta talk about white Vans for a moment—no, not the creepy automobile, the popular type of shoe. Going into my freshman year of high school as I started to rebrand my life around Jesus and what He said about me, I also wanted to change some things about my style in order to stand out a little bit more and have some fun with it (and no, these things aren't connected for every person, but for me they went hand in hand). So I told my mom, as we were shopping for new school shoes that year (which was an annual tradition for us), that I wanted a pair of all-white Vans.

She agreed. I got them. I rocked them on the first day of high school.

And guess what happened?

People made fun of them a little bit.

"You better not spill anything on those!"

"I can't see! Those vans are so white. It's blinding."

"Watch out! I might step on those brand-new shoes!"

You get the point. The list could go on.

But I decided that it didn't matter. I liked them. They made me feel cool and unique, and for me and my newfound confidence in Jesus, that was enough!

All I'm saying is this. In the month and even next year that followed, white Vans and white shoes of all kinds exploded. People at my high school were wearing white shoes more than any other color, and if you were to go to a high school today, you'd probably see the same thing. So I'm not going to sit here and say that I caused a monumental fashion trend to occur, but if the white shoe fits, wear it!

But in big ways, too, all throughout high school, I stayed true to what I felt like God wanted from me. I had a group of close friends, but I tried to make friends with just about everyone. People knew they could count on me to help them, talk to them, and just about anything that was needed, I would at least try to point them in the right direction if I couldn't directly help them out. I became friends with the athletes, the outcasts, the students with special needs, and everyone in between. People knew that I held myself to a different standard. They could hang out, talk, laugh, and do life with me, yet people knew that I didn't drink, smoke, talk bad about other people, or give in to some of the things that others did.

This cost me some friends, sure. This had people scratching their heads, maybe. But it fit perfectly into my desire to swim upstream and not be just a number. And guess what? I survived high school! Not only that, but since then, a couple times a year, I have people I graduated with reaching out to me, asking questions about Jesus and their faith. And the conversation usually starts with, "I just always noticed how different you were in high school."

That's one of the biggest compliments I can get because it means I reflected Jesus in some way.

Maybe you love being just a number. Maybe being behind

the scenes and in the background is your jam. And if that's the case, then in this area, you and I are very different. Which is totally okay! The ideas that I want to uncover in this chapter can speak to both groups of people at the same time. I'm not saying that following Jesus equals wearing white shoes and being louder in social settings. Following God isn't a one-size-fits-all type of thing. But what I am saying is I believe, when you really understand what Jesus has done for you, everyone else's opinions get a little quieter. I do think finding your identity in Jesus changes the game. But before we really get to why this matters, let's dive back into our story for a little while.

☥

What happened next may potentially scar your mind for the rest of your life.

The walk to Golgotha was downright terrifying.

People lined the streets and hurled insults, spit, and even rocks as your brother and the two other criminals carried their crosses through the city and up to the spot where the crucifixion would happen.

Your brother and his friend led the pack of three, but this Jesus character trailed a little bit behind because of how badly he had been beaten by the guards and officers. You're thankful that you didn't have to witness the beating because the results on this man's face and arms are brutal enough. At one point, it got so pitiful and slow that a man stepped in to help him carry the cross.

Your own brother was on this walk as well. So naturally he had the majority of your attention.

When they finally arrived at the spot where the execution was going to happen, you remembered learning about it at an early age in school. Golgotha. Some people referred to it as "The Skull," which is what the name means. Now, standing in its eerie presence, you understand why it was called this. The dark and ominous feeling that surrounded the entire hillside was enough to send chills up your spine, and you find yourself slightly unable to keep your balance.

What took place next happened in a flash. Your dad actually had you and your mom turn your back to the scene for a moment, but the noises and screams you heard painted a vivid enough picture in your mind.

The nails.

One through each wrist and an extra long one through the ankles. The noise as the hammer hit each time, of flesh and blood being pierced, was nauseating. You hear someone throw up to your left. The pounding of the hammer happens again. And again. And again. The crowd is so silent that the spray of blood and squelch of flesh is unavoidable. This really was the most brutal way to die.

After a few minutes of each of the three accused men going through this pain, they're lifted off the ground and up onto the crosses, where they each will take their last breath in a few short hours.

You turn around, and for the first time, you see your brother spread out in the crucifixion position. Three men: your brother on the left, his friend on the right, and this Jesus character in the middle. This sight is enough to take any strength you had left away from you. You suddenly begin to sob, and your entire body shakes with the intensity of your emotions. You collapse to your knees in despair.

This is more brutal than I was ready for, you think to yourself.

Suddenly, a newfound terror overtakes you—a realization of something that you had blocked out of your mind for a while, the realization that your brother's life was about to end and according to just about every law and belief that your family raised you to hold, he was going to Hell. Even though you are on the brink of not believing in God anymore, staring in the face of death here in this moment, the fear of Hell grips your heart.

Is he thinking the same thing? you wonder to yourself about your brother. *Is he gripped by this same fear that, in just a short time, he is going to find out what is on the other side of life?*

You begin to think through everything that your brother has done in the last couple years to see if there is any kind of redeeming quality in his life or any actions that could make him worthy of Heaven, but you come up short.

It's hopeless, you admit to yourself.

Suddenly, Jesus lets out a cry of anguish as he pulls himself up using the nails that are driven through his hands to say, "Father, forgive them, for they don't know what they are doing"

The crowd watched, and the leaders scoffed. "He saved others," they said, "let him save himself if he is really God's Messiah, the Chosen One." The soldiers mocked him, too, by offering him a drink of sour wine. They called out to him, "If you are the King of the Jews, save yourself!" A sign was fastened above him with these words: "This is the King of the Jews" (Luke 23:34-38, NLT).

Wait, what? you ask yourself. *This is the man that people have been talking about for months? At work? In the synagogue? Everywhere? This is the one who claims to be the Son of God? The awaited Messiah?*

You had heard so much about his teachings, following, and even miracles that you had often wondered if he could be the one that he was claiming to be. But because of your own family going through this crucifixion, you hadn't connected the dots.

Your brother's friend suddenly chimes in with laughter in his voice, "So you're the Messiah, are you? Prove it by saving yourself—and us, too, while you're at it!" (Luke 23:39, NLT).

In a matter of seconds, even milliseconds, after he said this, your brother pulled himself up a few inches and shot back in a tone that you hadn't heard from him before, "Don't you fear God even when you have been sentenced to die? We deserve to die for our crimes, but this man hasn't done anything wrong." Then he said, "Jesus, remember me when you come into your Kingdom" (Luke 23:40-42, NLT).

Your family watched in awe, jaws dropped, at what your brother had just said. Was he faking? Was this fear speaking? What was happening?

Jesus looks over at him from His place in the center of the crosses, and from where you're standing, you can see a little smile on his lips. It is one of complete love, even in the middle of His excruciating pain.

Finally, after a moment of this, Jesus replied, "I assure you, today you will be with me in paradise" (Luke 23:43, NLT).

Everything in your body goes numb as these words are spoken. Your mom begins to cry loudly. Your father falls to his knees on the ground while staring up at the two of them. Jesus then slumps down once again.

This cannot be real. Who does this guy think He is? What if it is real? What if He is the Son of God? Did my brother know? All of these questions race through your mind.

Your brother then turns his head and looks at the three of you standing below the crosses, and he smiles. Tears are streaming down his face.

In the middle of the most painful and worst moment of his life, he smiles—a smile that looked like all of his cares were gone, a smile that was full of newfound confidence.

His eyes then meet yours. Tears begin to well up in both of your eyes, and he smiles at you.

Then he winks.

Everything was going to be okay. Somehow.

Then, out of nowhere, the man named Jesus, who just told your brother he was going to Heaven, shouts into the sky, "My God, my God, why have you abandoned me?"

Complete silence falls over the entire crowd. There is no noise besides the labored breathing of the man left on the cross.

Woah.

✞

I want to talk about two different types of stains. My reason for this is that there are two different kinds that greatly impact and affect our lives for eternity. And no, I'm not talking about when you drop spaghetti on your brand-new t-shirt. I've been there, and it's a horrible feeling. Some of us have ruined more clothes than others. My wife, for example, has a not-so-great track record of dropping food on clothes. (Sorry, Lex, I had to go there.) But dropping food is irrelevant, so let's move on.

I want to clarify these two different types of stains because, if we can really understand what they are and why they matter, this will bring us into our conversation about being a number in a much more powerful way.

The first kind of stain that we all deal with is the stain of sin. We touched on this a lot in the first section of this book, so I won't spend too much time on it here, but it's important to bring it up once more because it's a universal issue, and there is no escaping it. You and I and every person who has ever walked planet earth (except Jesus who was the GOAT, or was He the Lamb?) are stained by sin. Due to sin entering into our DNA when Adam and Eve fell, we all have to deal with and rectify the natural bent we all have toward sin and separation from God.

We're stained. Humanity has this stain baked into who we are, and no amount of our attempts at course correction, Band-aids, homemade remedies, or trying hard enough can take that stain away or make it any less noticeable. We are all just a number in the billions and billions of stained human beings on this earth.

But there's one more type of stain that we have to bring into the conversation. This is where things get interesting. You see, this stain is an optional one (like if you chose to dump spaghetti on your white shirt that you're wearing to dinner, which is a terrible idea by the way). And this stain separates us from the type of humanity that we're born into. It changes our status from just a number to chosen by the Number.

Let me explain.

This good stain is the stain that remains after we're covered by the blood of Jesus, as we've talked about before. When we choose to believe in Him, we are then covered by His blood and elevated to a status of loved and accepted by God, which is something that we cannot earn on our own. The moment of believing in Jesus and accepting Him into your heart is almost like when the blood is poured onto your life, but then, when we go on living for Him after that initial moment, we're left with the stain.

Now, this stain shows up more visibly in some people's lives as compared to others. This doesn't mean that some people are more saved than other people, so let's not even go down that road and get into that argument.

What this means is that some people choose to look and act more like Jesus in their everyday lives than others. Some people choose to carry the message and love of Jesus with them no matter where they go. Their work. Their home. Their friends. Their marriage. Their singleness. Doesn't matter! They choose to exemplify Jesus to everyone that they come into contact with.

Their stain is extremely obvious.

This is how we should choose to live.

You see, when we truly understand the fact that something has gone missing in our lives, and we realize how mind-bogglingly awesome this really is, we will begin to prioritize that truth over everything else. I'm sorry! I went there. Some feelings may be hurt. But it's true.

When you really begin to understand and chew on the fact that the Son of God came to earth and died for your soul and rewired our path to Heaven, things change in your life.

"Well, I've just never been good at talking about this stuff."

"Well, I've just never been very smart, so I don't want to say the wrong thing."

"Well, in our world, it doesn't take much to get canceled, so I want to treat it lightly and accept everyone."

"Well, I just don't want to be pushy because people don't respond to pushyness."

Maybe you see yourself in one of these excuses. Maybe there's another one that you use to justify why you don't always live the way you feel like you should outside of church or Christian circles. Can I be brutally honest in a way that overtly religious people may not love?

It's all garbage.

Those excuses—your excuses, my excuses, the justification that we use to explain why we just don't share our faith with other people—is all bull absolute trash.

How can I be so sure of this?

Because I know that what our Savior has done for us is beyond worth sacrificing our reputation, time, and effort for if it means we can show our stain to other people. I know that we're not called to be perfect or know every word to say, but we are explicitly called to be faithful and obedient to God's Word. As far as I'm concerned, His Word calls us to be the salt and light of this earth (Matthew 5:13-16). His Word calls us to spread His image to the entire earth (Matthew 28:16-20). His Word calls us to deny ourselves and live for Him (Matthew 16:24-26). I could keep on going.

Stop being selfish with our Savior.

He didn't just die for you.

And He didn't die in secret.

Ready for a real gut check? Look at this.

"But everyone who denies me here on earth, I will also deny before my Father in heaven" (Matthew 10:33, NLT).

Ouch. These aren't my words, so don't be mad at me!

I have a feeling a lot of us are denying God every single day by the way that we choose to live, by the things that we talk about or don't talk about. We have got to get over ourselves and buy into the fact that Jesus is the most important thing.

Now, what does this have to do with being just a number? Great question.

Picture this with me. Let's pretend that I.D. cards worked a little bit differently in the world that we live in. Let's say that regardless of where you were born, what you looked like, or any other disclaimer that we want to add in there, you were given an I.D. the moment that you were born. And this wasn't just any old form of identification. This one we were all given was bought for a high price (one that we definitely couldn't afford, no matter how rich our families were). It allowed us to have extreme value, to be known by the most powerful people, and to have extreme luxury and riches in our lives and after we die.

But there's a catch.

The moment that you messed up, it was revoked. I'm talking like ripped to shreds and deleted from the system. For most of us, we messed up as a child before we even fully knew we were messing up. So, no matter how hard we tried, how good our parents tried to raise us, or the pressure that we felt was on our shoulders, by a couple months (or days or even minutes, as some new parents would say) into our new life, our awesome form of identification and status were ripped away from us.

Now, our status stayed this way—barren, empty, and somewhat useless, no matter how hard we worked, what connections we made, or how successful we were. All of humanity had this same issue. We could be working tirelessly toward changing our screwed-up status and never move the needle even an inch.

But there was a select group—not selected in the sense that they had access to something that no one else did, but select in the sense of the fact that the group wasn't very big. What made this group so different is that they were given I.D. at birth, had it taken away because they messed up, but then, eventually, got the same I.D. back. *How did they get it?* you ask.

By giving their old identity to someone else. Not only this, but they gave their time, energy, effort, worth, value, success, earnings, dreams, desires, heart, passions, plans, and even problems to someone else. This someone else took these things and redeemed their status to what they were born with, ensuring that the cost was already paid. They just had to trust this person with all that they had.

I don't know about you, but if this thing was real, I'd be doing everything in my power to find this person and give everything I have to them.

Well, that's exactly what Jesus is offering for all of us. But most people ignore it. Most people are missing out on an opportunity to live lives full of purpose and meaning because they can't see past the need to be successful by their own means.

Well, welcome to the life of just being a number.

Look around you. There are literally countless people striving, stressing, hustling, and doing more than ever before in order to come off as more successful, make more money, or keep the speed of our culture moving at a faster and faster pace. Odds are, if you look deep down into your heart, you're one of those people, adding to the speed, stress, and pace of the world. Sometimes, you may even feel like all your effort is in vain. Ouch.

In this world of just being a number, there is always someone better than you and always someone below you. If you're chasing this lifestyle, that reality can keep you up at night.

I need you to listen to me right here.

The One who has allowed something to go missing offers a different way—a way that directly works against speed, stress, doing rather than being, and working your life away. Now, before you close this book and disagree with what I'm saying, hear me on this.

Work is good. Work honors God. There is nothing wrong

with working hard and honoring God at your job and with your money. There is nothing wrong with climbing the corporate ladder or going to that prestigious college or getting that promotion.

As long as you keep the first things first.

Honor God first. Love Him and love others first. Find your identity in Him before anything else. Then, let God use you however He desires.

Most people don't have a problem with the belief that God created the world and all of the people in it. That's a relatively easy concept to get on board with. The harder concept for people to grasp is that God didn't just create the world and walk away, but He actually wants to be actively involved in our everyday lives and the things that we do. This is where a lot of people get tripped up because we all have a leaning (some more than others) to believe that we are doing things the right way, and we don't need anyone else's influence. We believe that our point of view is the best, and, in some ways, that it is the only point of view.

This is the problem of perspective.

We need to realize that each and every one of us is blind. In some way, shape, or form, we have blinders on to different things due to our sins, struggles, experiences, childhoods, and passions. And because of this, we need to humble ourselves, take a step back, and realize that we're not in control.

I'm an iPhone guy all the way. Prayers up for everyone who has chosen to live in sin and have Androids. So, whenever I'm using an Apple product, I fully trust the people who designed and created that product. I never have to question if they understand it better than I do. I know without a doubt that they do. So, when a new update comes out that says it will make it run faster, or a new tip comes out for using it better, I trust them!

Well, God designed you. He is the software developer of your heart and mind, and He knows them better than you do. When you read Scripture, and there are commands to stay away from things or to do other things, it is in your best interest to follow those. It's a pretty eye-opening shift to believe that God is actually on your team and not some grumpy old man upstairs just calling the shots because He's power hungry.

But one of those truths that is littered throughout His Word is the fact that we're not just a number. In fact, very much the opposite. When we give our lives to Jesus, we become children of God, and that's the only thing that should define us in our lives. Just look at some of the language used to describe you.

> "So God created human beings in his own image.
> In the image of God he created them;
> male and female he created them" (Genesis 1:27, NLT).

> "This means that anyone who belongs to Christ has become a new person. The old life is gone; a new life has begun!" (2 Corinthians 5:17, NLT).

> "You made all the delicate, inner parts of my body and knit me together in my mother's womb.
> Thank you for making me so wonderfully complex!
> Your workmanship is marvelous—how well I know it" (Psalm 139:13-14, NLT).

> "For we are God's masterpiece. He has created us anew in Christ Jesus, so we can do the good things he planned for us long ago" (Ephesians 2:10, NLT).

On your own, you're just a piece of humanity, but connected to the Master, you become a masterpiece.

Let that sink in for a moment. Stop and reflect on this section

SOMETHING IS MISSING

if you need to. It's not going anywhere. It'll be here when you get back.

The God of the universe holds you in a high place. This doesn't mean you should be cocky, arrogant, or prideful. But it does mean that you should find no greater value or worth from anything else on this planet except for this truth. When you really swallow and internalize this idea, everything else becomes secondary.

I don't know about you, but I'm completely okay with everything else failing in comparison to my love for God. Why? Because I'm well aware that everything fails in comparison to His love for me.

Have you ever been working on a puzzle that you're really excited to finish?

"No, Mitch. It's 2023. Most people don't work on puzzles anymore."

Okay, fair point, but at some point in your life, have you ever worked on a puzzle? Still no? Okay, do you know what a puzzle is? Awesome, let's go from there.

Most of the time, what the puzzle is going to look like is shown on the box that the pieces come in. So, the longer that you work on it and the more that you chip away at it, the more that the completed picture comes into view.

I'm partial to puzzles. Some of my favorite memories growing up were when my family would go on summer vacation or winter cabin trips, and my grandpa would sit at the giant kitchen table with a couple thousand piece puzzle and chip away at it every day. And as we were going to the pool or eating breakfast, we'd stop to help him. Sometimes, we would get sucked into the magic and fun of trying to complete this beautiful picture that was so broken.

But the most frustrating piece of doing a puzzle? When you get to the end and the picture is so close to being done, and there's a piece missing. You feel cheated and scammed. It makes you want to shove the whole thing down the garbage disposal and just go watch Netflix instead.

My brother, Rex, and his wife, Tori, got really into puzzles during the COVID-19 quarantine that we all found ourselves in a few years back. They ordered these really elaborate Star Wars puzzles, and three times in a row, the final piece was missing. It felt like someone at the company was playing a sick joke on them. It was kind of funny to me, but don't tell them I said that.

Jesus kind of operates like that worker at the puzzle company. When He is looking at the puzzle that is your life—so many different pieces, stories, memories, mistakes, questions, and people—it's almost as if He sees the beautiful completed picture on the box, but He removes one piece on purpose.

The piece He chooses to remove is the cost of your sin. He takes it out of the puzzle of your life and puts it down the garbage disposal the moment that you believe in Him. This piece is never to be seen again.

Why would Jesus do this? Because He's mean? Because He's pulling a sick joke? Why?

Well, because He knows the designer of the puzzle. And He knows that the picture is going to be a lot more beautiful without that piece. So He takes it upon Himself to remove it.

And that's what's funny about following God. It may not always make sense, but it is always worth it.

Jesus looks at the puzzle of your life that now has the missing piece of the cost of sin and says, "Aha! There's the masterpiece. It is finished."

Do you believe that?

KEY #4 -
YOUR IDENTITY HAS BEEN REDEEMED. YOU'RE NO LONGER JUST A NUMBER IN THE WORLD, BUT YOU'RE KNOWN, LOVED, CALLED, CHOSEN, PROTECTED, AND CONNECTED TO THE CREATOR OF THE UNIVERSE. NOT ONLY THAT, BUT THIS IDENTITY HAS BEEN EARNED AND GIVEN TO YOU BY JESUS! IT CANNOT BE TAKEN AWAY BY OUR MISTAKES. THIS FACT SHOULD MATTER MORE THAN ANYTHING ELSE! CHOOSE TO LIVE THAT WAY!

PART #3

#3

THE PROPOSITION

Chapter 9

YOUR PICTURE ISN'T COMPLETE, BUT HIS IS

The choice is yours.

After everything that we've traveled through so far in this book, this final section is going to offer a couple different ways for this book to come to life in your heart, no matter where you are in your walk with God. I've thrown out a lot of ideas, concepts, beliefs, and truths about the God of the Bible and how the blood of His Son Jesus has allowed for the cost of our sin to go missing. This is the only reason why you and I and anyone else in the world for that matter are able to go to Heaven when we die. It's not because we're good enough but because God is more than good enough. This is what this entire book has been built on, and I really hope that it's impacted the way that you think about God, other people, and yourself.

But—

I know full well how this goes. Some of you are sitting there and thinking to yourself, *Yeah this is great. You laid out some great ideas about God and stuff. But so what? How do I actually take these ideas and do something with them?*

Fantastic question.

That's what this final section is going to be all about—what to do with the incredible fact that something is missing in our lives. And not only what to do with it but what to do with it if you're in ministry, if you're a stay-at-home parent, if you're a nurse or a doctor or a school teacher, if you're an accountant or financial advisor or construction manager, if you're a follower of Jesus or you're on the fence or you're an atheist. What do you do with a book like this? Let's find out.

So far in this book, each chapter has ended with different things. The first section ended with "clues" (because we hadn't discovered what was missing yet, and we were still looking for it), and then "keys" (because we found what was missing but didn't know why it mattered or how to unlock it), and now "treasures" (because we've unlocked what is missing, why it matters, and now we need to find out how to live with the benefit or payment of it in our lives). Let's find some gold, baby!

The last stop of the journey is here.

Let's go!

✟

The sky goes dark.

Where did the sun go?

It was a bright and sunny morning just a moment ago, and now it was as if it were nighttime. You wonder if a storm had come upon the town that fast, but even then, you would've noticed the storm clouds before they were right on top of you.

There is a faint whisper of fear that ripples through the crowd of people who were still standing there.

What in the world is going on? you ask yourself.

Your family continues to watch as your brother's body slowly gives out. At one point, your dad shields you as his legs are broken. This is a common practice used to speed up the process of death. Over the period of a few hours, the suffocation takes over. Everything goes limp, and you hear his last breath leave his body.

That's the end.

It really happened.

Your family of four was now a family of three.

What now?

As the three of you stand there, unable to move, watching as the guards move your brother's body down from the cross that he had been on, you begin to shake, almost as if your body is in shock from watching all of this take place. You suddenly notice that your parents are no longer standing with you but have gone to recover your brother's body. You walk over to them as they're finishing wrapping him in cloth. Your father lifts him up and sets him on his shoulder to be carried back home.

"Are you ready to go?" your father asks you, barely keeping it together due to the fact that he was holding his own son's lifeless body on his shoulder. You nod and notice the guards have begun to retrieve the other two bodies from the crosses. Before anyone could move toward Jesus' body, still hanging on the cross, an earthquake started to disturb the entire city. Everything shook violently, and the noise was deafening. Rocks were splitting in half, and the people around you were ducking down to avoid falling over or being hit by the cracking rocks.

Could this be because He was actually the Son of God? you think to yourself as you get knocked off your feet and fall to the ground.

After the earth stops shaking and the people begin to pull themselves together, you quickly notice the fear that has overcome the guards and officials around you. There is a panicked whisper and a sense of nervousness that can be felt just by standing next to them.

You set your attention on one man, who is still sitting on the ground after being knocked down from the earthquake. He remains on the ground just staring up at the cross where Jesus' now lifeless body hung. His eyes are wide and jaw tight as he stares up. You wonder what he could be thinking.

He slowly stands to his feet, still staring at Jesus' body. You can see him swallow hard, almost as if he wants to say something but doesn't have the words quite yet.

Then, in a loud enough voice that a lot of the people still at the scene could hear, he shouts, "This man truly was the Son of God!" (Matthew 27:54, NLT).

You look at your parents as they look back at you. Confusion and disbelief fill their faces. If this man really was the Son of God, and He said those words to your brother, then that means he really is in Heaven, right?

Before you can fully process this question that is now running rampant inside your mind, the crowd begins to get a little bit more panicked and anxious due to the realization that the guards had made a mistake. What they had all witnessed wasn't justice. It was murder.

As your parents begin to understand that this crowd was growing more and more restless by the second, they look at each other, look at you, hoist your brother's body back up, and attempt to leave quickly.

You follow closely behind them, cutting in between so many people as they continue to stand there. Some are arguing. Some are crying. Some are even praying. But for you, it's a big mass of humanness where you are only catching bits and pieces of each conversation because your family is trying to get out of the area as fast as possible.

After you descend the hill where everything took place and begin to walk into downtown, you're shocked to see that there is just as much if not more panic there.

People are flooding the streets and trying to figure out what

SOMETHING IS MISSING

has happened. Someone even steps in front of your dad and asks if the body he's carrying is that of Jesus. Your dad shoves the man away, and your mom immediately bursts into tears.

The three of you continue to walk through the crowded and busy streets when you come to the Temple that is central in this town, and masses of people are gathered around its doors.

Your dad stops for a second at the sight of this and grabs a random bystander to ask, "Do you have any idea what's going on here?"

"Yeah, the whole town has lost its mind. Apparently, when the earth shook and things went wild here a little bit ago, the veil in the Temple was torn in half—top to bottom."

There are too many coincidences, too much chaos. This man really might've been the Son of God, you think to yourself.

✝

I told a lot of my story in my first book, so I'm not going to bore you with it here. Also, I never want to write a book about myself. The only reason I use personal stories is with the hope that they reflect God in some way or make an aspect of Him clearer for those who read these words.

But one aspect of my story and personality that is vitally important to my understanding of God is my constant drive for success. It's funny to me because the older that I get, the more this drive becomes even more obvious to me. A lot of things I do are motivated by the desire to succeed. The flipside is also true. I have a fear of failing or coming off as unimpressive.

I gotta work on that.

The more I reflect on my life and story, the more I see this everywhere. When I played soccer throughout my life, whenever I would mess up or get injured or let my coaches or parents down, it would destroy me. When I would score average on a test or assignment at school (which, by the way, my entire academic career could probably be summed up with the word average), it would fill me with nervousness and a headful of thoughts about how I wasn't good enough.

Not only this, but I grew up in church, and as I began to understand what it meant to have a relationship with God and follow Him every day, I started to develop the habit of journaling and reading my Bible and things like that, and whenever I'd miss a day of doing these things, I'd be full of so much guilt and worry that I had messed up and fallen short of what I was supposed to do.

To this very day, my life has been somewhat dominated by this fear that somehow and in some way, I am letting people down. Maybe you can relate to this, and maybe you can't.

But I'd argue that all of us have a desire to succeed in some way. Each and every one of us has a desire to please someone or something in our lives, and when we are unsure of how to do this or if we're doing it, it can really begin to mess with us.

This is why, as we bring this book to a close and focus on the question of how to live this out, I wanted to start with this question of success and pleasing God. How do we know when we're successful in this area? How do we know when we've done enough or lived in a way that God is proud of us?

This question becomes especially important once we've come to terms with what this book is all about. We realize that the God of the universe has allowed for something to go missing, and because of this, we can be made right in His eyes. If we needed any more convincing of the fact that God deserves our respect, worship, and service, this is it! Without His Son's sacrifice, we're unqualified, unworthy, and condemned. And the worst part? We're stuck in that spot indefinitely on our own. No matter how good we try to be or how many things we try to add to our Christ-like actions resume, we're stuck. The needle can't move even an inch based on our actions alone.

But we can be stuck on the other side of the spectrum as well. And this is a good kind of stuck. There's a popular idea floating around the church world in worship and preaching that states,

"You'll never be more loved than you are right now." Now, as cute and encouraging as this may sound, I also want to point out the fact that it's true. The disclaimer on this statement, though, is that it's true for those who have a relationship with Jesus and believe in what He's done on the cross. Because, for those who have decided to do so, they are covered by the blood of the lamb, something has gone missing, they've been made new, and now they can stand before God with no condemnation.

Scripture tells us,

> "The Lord is compassionate and gracious,
>   slow to anger, abounding in love.
> He will not always accuse,
>   nor will he harbor his anger forever;
> he does not treat us as our sins deserve
>   or repay us according to our iniquities.
> For as high as the heavens are above the earth,
>   so great is his love for those who fear him;
> as far as the east is from the west,
>   so far has he removed our transgressions from us"
> (Psalm 103:8-12).

Woah, woah, woah. If you can just skip over those words and they don't immediately bring thankfulness to the surface of your heart, you might want to read them again. Slower this time. Maybe even a third time.

Are you for real?

This God that we serve is gracious, slow to anger, and abounding in love. He doesn't always accuse and doesn't treat us as we deserve (thank the Lord because we deserve Hell). The psalm goes on to talk about how He is as a Father, and it's amazing news for us because He's a good Father. In fact, He's the best Father there's ever been.

When we believe in God's Son, Jesus, who gave up His life

for us on the cross and allowed for something to go missing, His love for us becomes the lens through which God sees us. Now, we can never be more or less loved than we are through the blood of Jesus. In Christianity, this is called justification. It's when we become justified or good enough because we've accepted what Jesus has done.

I mean, come on, we have to be immensely thankful for this! After all, we mess up. A lot. Daily. And if God's love for us was based on how good we were that day or how many times we didn't screw up, we wouldn't be loved very much. Not only that, but following God would be a roller coaster. His love would be up one day, down a lot the next day, up for a second, and down for a while. Throw in some loops somewhere. You get the picture: we'd be sick of it. And I'd imagine He'd be sick of us if it were possible for Him to feel that way.

But instead, because something has gone missing, the perfection of Jesus covers us, and we are brought into the family of God. His level of love for us doesn't change, even when we mess up. It's unconditional. It's never-ending. It's abounding.

We become stuck in His love.

And that's a very, very good place to be.

A couple months ago, I got stuck. Well, technically, I should say that my car got stuck. It wasn't a good place to be. In fact, I would say it was a pretty frustrating place to be.

Here in Ohio, we had a pretty bad snow storm. But what made it so bad is that in the days before the snow started, there was rain for a few hours, and then it turned into freezing rain, which lasted for almost an entire day. Then, with no hesitation, it turned into snow. So there was a decent amount of snow on the ground, but underneath it, there was a thick sheet of ice. Everywhere. It was also dangerously cold.

Plows couldn't get out because there was nothing they could do to the ice. We were unable to clear our driveways because the ice had gotten so bad. So, everyone just kind of stayed put for a couple days, which wasn't too bad. It was kind of relaxing, actually. But the problem was, I left my car out in the driveway. My wife and I just recently moved into our first house, so this was the first big winter storm that we'd encountered.

The day came when it started to warm up, and neighbors began trying to clear their driveways and cars in order to get back to life as we know it.

I went outside—tiny plastic snow shovel in hand, air pods in, ready to do this thing. I started at the bottom of the driveway and tried to clear some of the snow and ice, but I quickly realized something. Nothing would move. My plastic shovel looked like it was going to snap in half every time I used it, and the ice and snow weren't getting cleared at all.

So I moved on to my car. Now, what I need you to picture with me is all four wheels of my car being covered about halfway up with solid ice. All four sides of my car were boxed in by this ice sheet that covered the rest of my driveway. Under my car, I could see the blacktop of my driveway clear as day. Are you seeing the predicament here?

I started chipping away at the ice, but yet again, nothing moved. I have no clue how my shovel didn't break. I was kicking the ice around each tire and doing anything I could to break it up. I got in my car and threw the car in reverse and was revving the engine, trying to break out of the icy jail.

No movement. My car was frozen in my own driveway.

I was stuck.

I performed these steps three or four times over the next couple days, and nothing happened. Thankfully, we could take my wife's car to things when needed (because she gets the garage spot, but let's not go there right now. Love you, Lex, you're awesome), but when work came Monday morning, my car remained stuck in the same spot.

Finally, it came to my attention that what I was missing was a metal shovel. I was told by multiple people that the plastic shovel wasn't going to do what I needed. I ended up gaining possession of said metal shovel, and within a matter of minutes, my car was free and my driveway was completely clear.

The same thing happens when you step into a relationship with God and ask Him into your life. No matter how hard you tried before Him, the task is simply impossible. You remain stuck in your sin. But the moment that you trust in Him completely and believe in who He says He is, it's like He gives you the exact tool you need. Better yet, He clears it up for you! Now you're set free. Your chains are gone. Your identity is redeemed. You've been made new.

You're stuck in His love.

Now, here's where some of you may get bothered by me. Everything I just outlined about God's love for you is super encouraging. The fact that those who believe in Jesus will never be more or less loved based on our actions is a truth that should make us get up and dance with excitement. But there's one more thing we have to add.

This doesn't mean we can do whatever we want.

Here's where this conversation gets sticky (no pun intended) for some people. And the reason why it's so hard is because we live in a world that quite literally tells you the opposite. We live in a world that tells you to do whatever you want, be whatever you want, say whatever you want. You've heard these ideas before, right?

Live your truth.

Be the main character.

Blah blah blah.

These ideas are directly contradictory to Scripture.

By talking through these ideas, we're also going to circle back to the original question posed in this chapter of how do we love and serve a God who has done all of these things through His Son Jesus by allowing something to go missing. So here we go. Strap in.

There are two major things that I want to address for this

chapter in order for us to really grasp how to love and please God and also how to live like something has gone missing.

First and foremost, loving God means denying yourself. Oh snap. We're going there. If you claim to love God, and you want to love Him in a way that will please Him and line up with what the Bible has to say about loving Him, then it will be at the expense of yourself. In fact, you must love God more than yourself if you really want to live the way that Scripture has called us to.

Not buying it? Try these on for size.

"Then Jesus said to his disciples, 'If any of you wants to be my follower, you must give up your own way, take up your cross, and follow me. If you try to hang on to your life, you will lose it. But if you give up your life for my sake, you will save it. And what do you benefit if you gain the whole world but lose your own soul? Is anything worth more than your soul?'" (Matthew 16:24-26, NLT).

Still not quite there? No problem. Here's one more.

"But everyone who denies me here on earth, I will also deny before my Father in heaven" (Matthew 10:33, NLT). I know I used this one earlier, but it's just so good.

Wow are you kidding me, Jesus. You're going to deny us in front of God if we deny you on earth? Sounds like you're not messing around here.

And trust me, I get it. You may be asking, "Why would I do this? Why would I choose to deny myself and live for someone that I can't physically see?"

Go ahead and reread all of this book. The God of the universe who is perfect, just, and set apart from us, made a seemingly unfair decision in our favor to allow His only Son to die in our place so that the cost of our sin could go missing, and we'd be able to stand in relationship with Him no longer stained by our sin and therefore not be condemned to Hell for eternity.

I think the least we can do is submit our lives to Him. I think the least He deserves is us getting over ourselves and following Him with all that we are.

Believe me, I know this is hard. We live in a world and a cultural moment telling you to run after your own desires, passions, and wants. And God does want us to dream, create, and be passionate! But all of these things need to be submitted and given to Him first.

Paul writes this in the book of Galatians, "My old self has been crucified with Christ. It is no longer I who live, but Christ lives in me. So I live in this earthly body by trusting in the Son of God, who loved me and gave himself for me" (Galatians 2:20, NLT).

I'd argue that many of us can't say those words with confidence the way that Paul writes them. I think most of us are still living for ourselves: in small ways like choosing to gossip, talk bad, or judge other people, and in large ways like choosing not to go to church (God's bride and mission) or serve others (what every single one of us is called to do if we claim to love God).

I think this is a huge problem.

We need to get over ourselves.

The world doesn't revolve around us.

God doesn't revolve around us.

We should revolve around Him.

Second, when you truly understand what has gone missing and you believe in what Jesus has done, you begin to change from the inside out. Plain and simple.

"This means that anyone who belongs to Christ has become a new person. The old life is gone; a new life has begun!" (2 Corinthians 5:17, NLT).

This statement comes from a passage where Paul is explaining that if you understand how game-changing Christ's love and sacrifice really is, you'll begin to live as if you're controlled by Christ's love. Now, everything you do, say, and even think is dominated by the fact that the Savior of the world thought the world of you.

He even goes on to say that this changes how we view other people. We see them as people created by God, and we know that they need to hear the same message of Jesus and how something has gone missing, so they don't spend eternity separated from God.

But the main point that I want to pull from Paul's words is this idea of change. When you believe in God's Word, and you understand what Jesus has done for you, you change! You begin to see the world differently, and the way that you live reflects this. There is no way around this! When you accept the truth of Jesus, the Holy Spirit begins to go to work in your heart, and you enter into a journey of sanctification. "What is that?" you ask. Great question! Sanctification is the process of becoming more and more like Jesus and being molded into His image. And since we're all not Jesus, that means some things are going to have to change!

Now, some people go to church (or claim that they do) and say that they believe in God, yet they are living and acting the exact same way as before they ever heard His name or the gospel message.

Do they really know Jesus?

It's never our place to judge anyone's heart. That's God's role, so let's leave that to Him (yes, even those of you judging others on Facebook. Give it up, already, keyboard warriors). But I would argue that those who are really saved and set free by the blood of Jesus change their ways. Each and every day, they try to look more like Jesus and reflect more of His love to those around them.

Not only this, but they're intentionally pursuing what the Word of God actually says and learning how to follow God's commands.

Fine, let's get real for a moment. How do you know that you may be living for yourself or not truly changed by the blood of Jesus? Here are some excuses that you may see yourself in.

"I love Jesus; I just don't love church."

"Well, no one is perfect."

"Serving really isn't my thing."

"I know God loves me. Isn't that enough?"

"That's just who I am!"

"I just don't want to be uncomfortable or make others uncomfortable with my faith."

I could go on and on, but hopefully you get my point. Stop living for yourself, and start living for the God who gave up everything for you.

So, how do we love this God who gave His Son for us? How do we serve this God who made this (from our human point of view) unfair decision in our favor?

Jesus says, "If you love me, obey my commandments" (John 14:15, NLT).

Get in God's Word. Learn what it says. Figure out who this God is and what He's asking you to do (and not do). Realize that this God is good and removes the weight of our sin if we believe in Him. Stop trying to measure up and perform in a way where God is going to be proud of you. Just submit your life to Him because He knows better than you, and live in a way that is humble, thankful, and worshipful.

That's how we love a God who has allowed something to go missing for our sake.

TREASURE #1 -
WHEN WE LOVE GOD MORE THAN OURSELVES, WE WILL QUICKLY FIND TRUE JOY, PEACE, AND LIFE. WE NEED TO STOP MAKING EXCUSES, STOP BEING SELF-CENTERED, AND START DISCOVERING IN GOD'S WORD WHAT HE CALLS US TO DO. AND WHEN ALL ELSE FAILS, WE NEED TO FILL OUR LIVES WITH MORE THANKFULNESS AND WORSHIP BECAUSE OUR GOD HAD EVERY RIGHT TO CANCEL US BUT DIDN'T! WE ARE STUCK IN HIS LOVE! LET IT CHANGE US FROM THE INSIDE OUT.

Chapter 10

LIVING FROM ACCEPTANCE, NOT FOR IT

Have you ever had one of those moments?

I know. That was super descriptive. But I'm talking about one of *those* moments—you do something, say something, or even go somewhere, and shortly afterward, you realize the real reason why you did it? And it kind of stops you in your tracks because something small actually had a much bigger reason behind it?

Maybe for you it happened when you were out with friends, and you made that one joke. Everyone laughed, and it felt good in the moment. Then, later that night or the next day, you realize how mean the joke really was, and it hits you that you were just doing it for approval.

Maybe for you, it's not that deep. Maybe you ordered something at a restaurant that you really didn't want to eat just because the group you were with might've judged you if you got what you really wanted.

SOMETHING IS MISSING

For me, one of the most vivid memories I have of this was on the soccer field. I grew up playing soccer, and I loved playing the sport for many years of my life. I still do to this day, but due to some kneecaps that found their way to the back of my leg, it doesn't happen often. But that's a story for another time!

When I was younger and just started playing soccer more competitively, I can recall a few things so vividly that it's like they happened yesterday: when I scored my first goal in travel soccer (I can picture it in my head like a movie), getting to travel for a soccer tournament that was far enough away to stay at a hotel for the first time, and looking at my dad in the middle of the game.

Wait, what?

Maybe some of the athletes can relate to this memory. But for me, I will never forget the habit that I formed very early on in my competitive soccer playing days where I would look at my dad after every single play that I was involved in. It didn't matter the stakes of the game or even if I knew yet whether what I did was good or bad. I'd touch the ball. The play would be over. I'd look to the sidelines where he was standing.

Every single time.

"Why?" you may ask. Well, at first, I didn't know why. I became conscious of the fact that I was doing it, and I couldn't stop myself. It wasn't until I was much older that I realized why I did this (and yes, I stopped doing it, eventually).

It was because I was seeking his approval, which I think is pretty natural for most people who grow up competing or doing things to please their parents. I'd argue that we all have something deep within us that craves the head nod from a parent or a thumbs up from someone that we love.

For me, this carried itself out in my early days of playing soccer. I craved my dad's approval in this small way. Time and time again, I'd look at him after every play. I'd see his body language, his facial expressions, if he was even facing the field I was playing on anymore—all of the above. I just wanted to know what he thought.

And don't worry, this didn't last forever. I didn't live the rest of my life trying to earn my dad's approval or come off as good enough to him. I know some people are forever trapped under the weight of trying to please parents, and I can't imagine how disheartening this must feel. But for me, this didn't last forever. What changed?

I realized that my dad loved me for me. I understood that my dad saw me as more than my accomplishments and abilities. He saw me as so much more than what I could do on the soccer field. He loved me as his son. Yes, of course he wanted me to succeed and work hard and make him proud (as any dad does). But at the end of the day, he was proud of me already because I'm his son. I started to see this side of my dad with all of my siblings. With my entire family! And I'm from a big family.

Let me just say that this changed my entire perspective. It changed my dad's and my relationship, and it changed the way I viewed God. I began to understand, through my dad's example, that God isn't seeking perfection and waiting for the moment that we mess up. He's gracious, He's kind, He's slow to anger, and He loves us, His children, because we're His.

So, thank you, Dad. Let me know when you read this part just so I can thank you again.

✞

The veil in the Temple had been torn in half. What are the odds? The ultimate symbol of God being far away and removed from humanity had been ripped completely in half, top to bottom, the day, even the moment, that the supposed Son of God died.

It was all too real. It was all too convenient. And it was really hitting you hard.

But nothing, absolutely nothing, could prepare you for what came next. As your family continued their walk through town

SOMETHING IS MISSING

toward home, yet again you dodged so many people and heard tiny pieces of what felt like a million different conversations.

At one point, you saw a man surrounded by other people, and the other people were demanding, "So you were a disciple of this man? Tell us more! Is He really who He claims to be? Tell us now!"

You became so fixated on that scene for a second that your eyes stayed there, but your feet kept moving. You didn't notice that your mom had stopped walking in front of you, and before you knew it, you ran right into her back.

"Mom, I'm so sorry. I wasn't paying attention," you say to her, but you quickly notice that she isn't listening. You're not even sure if she noticed that you ran into her.

You peer around her, and what you see through the crowd is very strange. You see a woman who appears to be your mom's age, hugging an older woman who is covered in dirt, and even from where you're standing, you can smell her. It isn't a great smell.

"But Mom," the younger of the two women says, "it's been eight years since you passed away. How is this possible?"

Wait what?! you ask yourself. *There has to be a mistake. There is no way this is happening.*

You are unable to hear the rest of the conversation due to the people behind and around you being loud and excited. As you start to look around, you actually begin to see a handful of people covered in dirt and looking very similar. Some look lost as they walk through the city streets. Some are hugging and talking to supposed friends and family.

A couple walks behind you, and you hear the woman say, "What do you mean you think it's a lie? You saw the cemetery for yourself!"

The cemetery? What does that have to do with this? you wonder.

Your dad motions to your mom and you to continue walking. You follow him as the three of you cut around more crowds and continue in the direction of home.

After a couple more minutes of slipping in and out of people, trying to keep up with your family, you see the cemetery off in the distance and try to make out what is happening there. There are, yet again, so many people gathered around its gates that it's hard to make anything out at first.

You continue to peer and look and move around people until you see it.

The graves are empty. They look like they've been dug up, and now, there are large piles of dirt and empty holes that remain in their place.

Did someone steal the bodies? What is happening?

Then you connect it all. The dirt people. The women saying it's been eight years. The smell.

These people had come back from the dead.

This could not be real.

Nothing like this has happened before.

As you continue to process and try to understand what has happened, if this Jesus person is real, and everything in between, you find yourself at your front door.

Home at last.

Except this time as a family of three.

And despite all of the unbelievable and weird things that you saw that pushed your limits and even amazed you, this is the feeling that remains—the cold, numb, weird, empty feeling that your brother was gone.

As you walk in through the front door of your house, your dad sets the body in his former room and then embraces your mom, and they both break into tears. What a long, exhausting, emotional, terrible day.

This Friday will forever be burned into your memory. And how could it not be? The amount of stuff that has taken place could fill books.

It was a terrible, bitter, sad, dark Friday.

How could anyone ever say anything good about this Friday? you think to yourself as the emotions set in for you once again, and you give in to the sobs that overtake your body.

☦

I hold the belief that identity is one of the most important things we can talk about.

We live in a world where the conversation about identity and how you identify is taking over the culture. Everyone everywhere is searching for an identity and a group to belong to, and I think, as Christ-followers, if we can learn where identity really comes from and learn how to communicate that to the world around us, we can change the game.

In ministry and leadership, I am always seeking to define the "why" behind what is happening. If I can get leaders, students, whoever to identify their "why" behind what they're doing, it makes everything click.

I believe identity is a big source of "why."

I think the way you see yourself or what makes you *you* is extremely important. And I think it leads us to either do or not do certain things in life.

For me, I didn't know my identity until the summer before freshman year. When I found it, I found my "why."

I think maybe this chapter can help you do the same. Let's start with this.

How you see God defines how you see yourself. Even if you're reading this right now, and you're not entirely sure if you believe in this God, that still factors into how you see yourself.

Do you see God as an invisible dictator in the sky, waiting to strike you dead? If so, you may see yourself as small (in an unhealthy way) and useless and even fearful of messing up because you're nervous of falling short.

Do you see God as nonexistent? You don't believe in Him, and therefore, you see Him as a fairytale or a myth. If so, then you see yourself as the definer of truth, and your life is the only thing that really matters to you. Because, after all, there is nothing after this life or after you pass away, so you strive to make as many things serve you and make you happy. In a summed-up way, you see yourself as God. This obviously impacts your identity.

Do you see God only as your best friend? Do you think of God as following along with whatever life decisions you make or what the rest of the world is telling you to do? If so, then odds are you live however you want and always return to a place of "God loves me, so everything is fine!" And although the sentiment may be true, if you're living for yourself, then the question isn't about God's love for you; it's, "Do you even love Him?"

Do you see God as a vending machine? Whatever you want can just be "typed in" to Him, and it'll fall into your lap? If so, then life may be good at times, but the moment that God's plan doesn't line up with yours, and life gets in the way of the picture-perfect life you're creating, you'll have no reason to trust in God anymore.

Do you see God as good? When you read about Him, see Him at work in people's lives, read His Word, do you see all of His ways and His character as good? If so, then you'll be willing to live in a way that follows His commands and seeks after His leading because you know that you're being led by a good God who has your best interests in mind (especially since He designed your best interest and your mind).

Do you see God as the Creator and Author of life? If so, then you're probably a little bit more likely to be intimidated and fearful of Him (in a good way) because you see how wonderful and powerful He is. And odds are that this makes you more willing to walk with Him and trust His leading because you are submitted to Him.

Do you see God as the Designer of the world and the galaxies? If so, then nature probably speaks to you and constantly calls you back to gratitude for God and thankfulness that there's breath in your lungs each day to experience the good in every day.

How you see God defines how you see yourself.

So how do you see God?

When I was in seventh and eighth grade, I was chasing after popularity. Not running after. Not pursuing. Straight up chasing. Sprinting. Fighting for. Consumed by. You get the picture.

And years later, I realized I was sprinting after popularity and people's approval because I didn't see God the right way.

I was clawing and trying to get my friends and peers to like me because I wasn't aware that the Creator of the universe liked me and that was enough. It got so bad that I would be in the cafeteria cussing up a storm and talking bad about everyone around our table, and then I'd get up, walk to the next class, and sit with a group of people from youth group, and we'd be the nicest ones in the class.

My identity was fractured, and I was trying to please all of these different groups and people around me.

It was exhausting.

It was tiring.

It was hard to keep up with.

But then, I saw God in a new way.

And it finally clicked how God saw me.

Then I realized that how you see God defines how you see yourself.

This changes everything. Hopefully, for some of you reading this book, I've painted a picture of God (using God's Word and the ways that God defines Himself) to help you better see who this God is. Yes, He's all powerful. Yes, He's perfect. Yes, He's holy and set apart. Yes, He's just. Yes, He is God and therefore deserves all of our respect and worship.

But He's also good. Not only is He all of the things above, but He's good, and this changes everything about Him. When we see Him as good and forgiving and never-ending in love, it changes how we approach Him. When I see that the Bible is His way of protecting me and offering me true joy and peace, it changes how I approach it. When I see people around me as children of God and created by God, it changes how I love them.

You see how radical this shift is?

Then we flip the script and get to the other side of this conversation.

Step one is learning how to see God based on how the Bible describes and writes about Him. Step two is discovering what He has to say about you. So far in this book, we have established that we are all sinners who fall short of God's standards, and unfortunately, no matter how hard we try or how many good things we do, we are still sinners, and this truth is baked into our DNA.

But there's more to it than that.

God has allowed for something to go missing: the cost of our sin. Now, we can be made new if we believe in His Son, Jesus.

Does this mean we'll never sin again? Well, no. Not at all. We sin all the time. And we need to be constantly learning how to improve and walk closer with Jesus (more on that in the final chapter), but it does mean that we're no longer helpless sinners stuck in our position of brokenness.

When something went missing, our identity found a new definition.

Maybe the reason you lack confidence in who you are is because you lack knowledge of who God says you are.

The Creator of the universe has a lot to say about you, His child. When we truly believe that God sees us this way, and we see God as good and in charge, everything changes.

So what does this God say about us?

For starters, we are God's masterpiece because something has gone missing and has allowed for us to be born again.

"For we are God's masterpiece. He has created us anew in

Christ Jesus, so we can do the good things he planned for us long ago" (Ephesians 2:10, NLT).

Not only that, but we're loved. And yes, you're a part of the world.

"For this is how God loved the world: He gave his one and only Son, so that everyone who believes in him will not perish but have eternal life" (John 3:16, NLT).

You are chosen and called by this God.

"But you are not like that, for you are a chosen people. You are royal priests, a holy nation, God's very own possession. As a result, you can show others the goodness of God, for he called you out of the darkness into his wonderful light" (1 Peter 2:9, NLT).

God dwells within you. You are His temple. This all-powerful God wouldn't just live anywhere! That's saying something about us.

"Don't you realize that all of you together are the temple of God and that the Spirit of God lives in you? God will destroy anyone who destroys this temple. For God's temple is holy, and you are that temple" (1 Corinthians 3:16-17, NLT).

You're new. Let that sink in. When something goes missing, you are made new. The old is gone.

"This means that anyone who belongs to Christ has become a new person. The old life is gone; a new life has begun!" (2 Corinthians 5:17, NLT)

The victory is yours—victory over what you're facing and what you're going through—because the ultimate victory was already won through the death of Jesus.

"No, in all these things we are more than conquerors through him who loved us" (Romans 8:37, NIV).

You're made in the image of God. You're not an accident. You're not a screw-up. You're made in the image of the Creator of the universe. Think about that the next time you look in the mirror.

"So God created mankind in his own image,

in the image of God he created them;
male and female he created them" (Genesis 1:27, NLT).

You're God's light to this dark world.

"You are the light of the world—like a city on a hilltop that cannot be hidden" (Matthew 5:14, NLT).

You're a child of God.

"For you are all children of God through faith in Christ Jesus" (Galatians 3:26, NLT).

This God knows every piece of you and has designed it to be used for His glory, even the parts you don't like or that the world tells you not to like.

"You made all the delicate, inner parts of my body
and knit me together in my mother's womb.

Thank you for making me so wonderfully complex!

Your workmanship is marvelous—how well I know it" (Psalm 139:13-14, NLT).

You're never alone. When you believe in Jesus and what has gone missing, you become a part of the body of Christ (the church) and are now forever unified in a much bigger story than you could ever imagine.

"All of you together are Christ's body, and each of you is a part of it" (1 Corinthians 12:27, NLT).

You're empowered, bold, confident, and strong because of who God has made you to be and allowed you to be.

"For God has not given us a spirit of fear and timidity, but of power, love, and self-discipline" (2 Timothy 1:7, NLT).

You're free.

"He is so rich in kindness and grace that he purchased our freedom with the blood of his Son and forgave our sins" (Ephesians 1:7, NLT).

You are a masterpiece, loved, chosen, God's temple, a new creation, a conqueror, made in the image of God, the light of the world, a son or a daughter of God, fearfully and wonderfully made, known, united, empowered, bold, confident, redeemed, set free, and new.

This list sounds pretty good, if you ask me.

This list is available to you; you just have to accept it.

When this list of what God says about you takes root in your heart, everything else becomes secondary. When you know who the God is that created you, and then you discover what He says about you, what else matters?

When I was made aware of how much this God has to say about me and how, on my own, I wasn't able to be any of these things, but because something has gone missing, I can be all of them—I was never the same.

I'm hoping the same is true for you. I'm hoping and praying that, as you're reading this chapter, you can see, for the first time, what God has to say about you. Maybe, you can remind yourself of who you are in God. Because, if that's the outcome, I believe we are going to become more confident and unashamed of what Jesus has done for us. We'll no longer be living for the approval or opinions of others, but we'll have God's opinion of us tattooed on our hearts.

When God's opinion is tattooed on your heart, nothing else deserves your dedication.

That's why this conversation on identity matters so much. You are always identified by something. You are always searching to belong somewhere or identify with something or someone. How you choose to identify shapes the way you talk, think, act, and live.

And let me say this, choosing to identify with anything other than the One who created you is going to lead to frustration, anger, sadness, hurt, brokenness, hopelessness, and feeling lost. Why? Because everything we do apart from being rooted in Jesus leads to these things.

Why not identify with the One who created you and knows you better than you know yourself?

In John 8, Jesus is being questioned by the Pharisees (classic), and they are trying to figure out if who He says He is is valid.

They want to know if the testimony about His identity is true. Look at Jesus' response to them.

"Jesus answered, "Even if I testify on my own behalf, my testimony is valid, for I know where I came from and where I am going. But you have no idea where I come from or where I am going" (John 8:14, NIV).

Confidence. Boldness. True identity. Jesus knew where He came from and where He was going. Do you?

Shoutout to Anthony Rex for always talking about the importance of identity with me and showing me verses like this one, where Jesus speaks on knowing who we are.

Are you confident enough in who Jesus died for you to be and who God created you to be to know where you came from and where you're going? We all came from a place of sin and brokenness. We're all going either toward Heaven or Hell. And we're taking people with us by the way that we choose to live.

Which side of eternity are you crowding?

Heaven or Hell?

It all depends on if you know who you are, and where you're going.

When I was a kid, playing soccer, I looked at my dad for approval. Every time I would touch the ball or make a play, I would search for his approval. When he was clearly angry, and the approval wasn't there, I was a mess! I was unable to focus on the rest of the game because all I could think about were my mistakes.

Don't do the same thing to God.

If you're constantly looking to God to see if He approves of you, and if what you did was good enough, the moment that you mess up (which won't take too long to happen), you will be so distracted and thrown off that you may miss opportunities to serve Him or love others right in front of you.

Stop trying to earn your approval. Jesus already did that for you.

It's time to live with the confidence that we have God's

approval and not with the deficit of constantly wondering whether we do. One leads to freedom. The other leads to distraction.

When you sin, pray to God, and ask for forgiveness. Know that He hears you and because of Jesus allowing something to go missing, He freely forgives you. Get closer to God in the process.

That's it.

How much more effective would you be if, instead of constantly looking at God on the sidelines, wondering if what you did was good enough, you understood that His Son, who was more than good enough, died in your place to set you free? What if you lived in that confidence and truth instead?

I would imagine we'd start to look a lot more like Jesus, knowing where we've been and where we're going.

TREASURE #2 -
WE CAN HAVE CONFIDENCE AND ASSURANCE IN WHO WE ARE BECAUSE OF WHO GOD IS AND WHAT HE SAYS ABOUT US. WE NO LONGER HAVE TO SEEK OR CHASE AFTER GOD'S APPROVAL BECAUSE WE UNDERSTAND FULL WELL THAT GOD APPROVES THOSE WHO HAVE BEEN SET FREE BY THE BLOOD OF JESUS. IF WE BECOME ROOTED IN THE IDENTITY JESUS HAS EARNED FOR US, IT CHANGES THE WAY WE TALK, THINK, TREAT OTHERS, AND LIVE OUR LIVES EVERY SINGLE DAY.

Chapter 11

THE NEVER-ENDING DISCOVERY

I love Easter.

Are there any holidays for you that you loved as a kid and that you continue to love more and more, every year that you experience them? The older that you get, you still find more ways and reasons to love that holiday?

For me, Easter is one of those.

I loved it as a kid, and then, once I realized how much it meant, I loved it even more and continue to find new reasons to love it every year.

It's just the best.

As a kid, we had a tradition that my grandparents would do for us every single year. The good ol' Easter egg hunt. They'd bring a bag full of eggs, and the eggs would be divided up based on how many kids were finding them that year. So, before we'd start, our parents would say to us, "Okay you can only find ten. Once you get to ten, help the younger kids find theirs."

But there was a catch. This wasn't just any ordinary Easter egg hunt. The eggs didn't have candy in them.

They were full of money.

Oh yeah. It got intense.

Most of the eggs would have a dollar or two in them. Some of them would be quarters, some dollar bills, but there were a very select few out there that would have five-dollar bills and maybe even a $10, depending on the year.

As a ten-year-old boy, this was the time to make some extra money. I couldn't get a job yet, but I could beat my younger nieces and nephews to the best eggs!

I'll never forget the year I turned fourteen, and I was told I was too old for the Easter egg hunt. I couldn't believe it. I was being laid off from my only part-time job. It was ridiculous. Something about budget cuts was shared, but I was too upset to listen.

But then, something changed. After being told that I was too old to find the eggs anymore, it was followed up with, "But now, you get to hide the eggs and make the experience more fun for the younger ones."

I could get into this, I thought to myself.

That year, I started hiding eggs in the most unique and fun places and then walking through the hunt with the younger ones in my family, giving them hints and helping them find the eggs that I had hidden.

Even though my time of finding the eggs myself was over, I learned to help the rest of the kids in my family still enjoy finding and discovering them. It became a never-ending discovery. Either I was finding them or hiding them and assisting on the journey.

What if God has called us to follow the same design?

One of the most dangerous ways to live your life and conduct your faith is to fall into the trap of believing that you've somehow "arrived." What I mean by this is that when you think you're good enough or you've made it, you stop trying. You stop improving. You stop learning. You stop growing. And I believe that when we're not actively walking toward Jesus, we're walking toward something else.

Our hearts are always worshiping and gravitating toward something. Doesn't matter if you're an atheist who doesn't believe in God, you're worshiping something. Doesn't matter if you've gone to church your entire life, you may not be worshiping God, but you are worshiping. It's not a matter of if, it's a matter of what.

And this is why this book has to end on the conversation around the never-ending discovery of Jesus that needs to happen every single day.

Jesus didn't allow for something to go missing so that you would go to church. Jesus didn't allow for something to go missing just so you would check "Christian" on a survey or put a Bible verse in your Instagram bio.

Hopefully this book has shown you the vital importance of what Jesus did on the cross and how something is missing so that you can live freely. I don't know about you, but if all of this is true, and the Son of God died so that the debt could be paid, and not only that, but it was the only payment option available, then I have no other option but to follow God with all that I have.

Who am I to deny God or live for myself once I've seen the immeasurable price that was paid on the cross through the unfair decision that was made in my favor?

Following Jesus and walking alongside Him is a never-ending discovery.

You may be wondering something along the lines of, "How is it never-ending? I've heard everything I need to hear about Him. I even read through this book, for crying out loud? So what is there to discover?"

Well, that's a good question. Hopefully you didn't ask it as aggressively as I wrote it, but either way, this truly is never-ending in a few different ways.

First and foremost, it's a never-ending discovery because we're called to be perfect as God is perfect.

Now, before you panic and chuck this book out your back door, hear me out. Yes, you are called to be perfect. Even with all your brokenness and mess-ups and the fact that you sin and fall short of God's standard every single day, you're still called to be perfect.

Doesn't this contradict pretty much everything that we've said up until this point because Jesus has allowed for the weight of our sin to go missing? Aren't we free from condemnation and God's judgment? But now we're called to be perfect, so how do those two things exist at the same time?

Let's take a look at what Jesus says on this.

Jesus is sitting in front of a crowd during His "Sermon on the Mount" and is walking through how to follow God in a handful of different areas of life. He's outlining what it truly looks like to follow God in relationships, hardships, and all kinds of things. It's potentially His most famous and longest teaching that's recorded in the Bible.

But in Matthew 5, toward the end of the chapter, Jesus begins to talk about how we're called to love our enemies. You know that one? It usually doesn't make us feel too good about ourselves because we struggle with it.

Jesus is explaining how it's not hard for us to love those who love us back. He even says that anyone can do that, so why do we assume that's what we're being called to do? But He says to really live out the way that God calls us to live, we should love those who are our enemies and pray for those who are against us.

Ouch, right?

And then, He says this as the chapter comes to a close, "But you are to be perfect, even as your Father in heaven is perfect" (Matthew 5:48, NLT).

Now, I went ahead and searched just about every translation that I've heard of, and you know what just about all of them say? The word perfect.

It seems like such a big idea that Jesus packs into a one-sentence mic drop moment. But you and I are called to be perfect as God is perfect.

Anyone else feeling a little bit nervous?

What did Jesus mean by this?

The Greek word translated as perfect here is "teleios," which means a state of maturity or wholeness. Lacking nothing. What Jesus is saying here when He's talking about how our love should be isn't a call for us to never make mistakes but rather a call for us to mature in our faith and continue to grow to be like Him. The New Testament even goes on to talk a lot about this idea of spiritual maturity and how to get there.

God's heart for you is maturity.

And the process of maturity is a never-ending discovery.

Why? Because we're human, and to be quite honest with you, we're not going to get to a place in our lives where we are fully like Jesus. It just isn't going to happen! There's a reason why Jesus walked this planet two thousand something years ago, and there hasn't been anyone like Him since. We are broken, flawed, human people with sin inside our DNA.

But because the example is Jesus, who was perfect and lacking nothing, then you and I have a target that we can work toward every single day. We can always find ways to love more (worry less), talk more, learn more, share more, and be more like Him. Giving our lives to Jesus and having a relationship with Him means committing ourselves to the never-ending discovery of becoming more like Him. We are called to a place of maturity.

Are you still acting like a child? Do you still want everything to serve you, be convenient, be easy, and look out for you first? I'm not knocking on babies here, but naturally, that's how they act! They're not taught to be selfish; they just are! But they have to be taught to be selfless. In a few short months, my wife and I are about to walk through the process of raising a baby for the first time. But I don't have to have my own child yet to know that I've grown up a little since I was born!

Have you? Are you still acting like a child? Or are you moving toward maturity in Jesus? Because when you stop moving toward one, you begin to walk toward the other.

Not only this but doing life with the Son is also a never-ending discovery because you can never learn or know enough about Him. There is always more to learn! In this story of God and us, we will always be the students, and anyone who pretends or believes that they know it all is wrong and maybe even arrogant!

There is always room to learn more about God. Every time you open His Word or pray to Him, it's an opportunity to hear more from Him and understand Him even better. This is another reason why daily time with Him and in His Word is vitally important to the way that we live because it shows us even more about who He is, the types of things He says and asks of us, and how we can faithfully respond.

I'm fully convinced that we will never trust yet alone follow a God that we don't know. We will never trust in a God that we don't know cares for us and about us. It just won't happen!

I hope this book has been a tool for understanding this God better, but it's not gospel. It's not the Bible. The Bible is the Bible. Nothing can replace or outdo it. It's the Word of God and speaks to every single situation and problem we could find ourselves in. Not only that, but it reveals who this God is: His character, His story, and why He's worthy of our praise and worship.

The Word of God is vitally important to following God.

In fact, this God is nearly impossible to follow if you don't first accept the Bible as truth. Cover to cover. Inside and out. Genesis to Revelation.

I think so many of us are claiming a relationship with a God that we barely know. That's so sad. Since the beginning of time, He's had a desire to know you, and He even made a seemingly unfair decision for you so that your sin wouldn't disqualify you from knowing Him! But we can't give Him the time of day—literally the time out of our day.

Imagine a relationship between two people where they didn't talk. They decided that it would be best to never speak to each other. In fact, they've never heard each other's voices.

It sounds like a really frustrating plot for a rom-com or something.

We do the same thing to God when we choose to follow Him yet don't spend time reading His Word or communicating with Him in any way. How are we going to know if He's speaking? If He's leading? If He's calling us? If He's in control? If we don't even know the types of things He'd say or the type of God He is?

It's really pretty plain and simple: we won't.

But not even all of this. The script flips as well.

Just like an Easter egg hunt, once you discover the eggs for yourself, it then becomes time to hide eggs for the other people in your life.

Don't keep the ultimate Easter egg of Jesus hidden to yourself.

If you're someone who has a relationship with God, then odds are there were people along the way who helped you lay that foundation and make the decision to follow Him. Maybe they invited you to church. Maybe they bought you a Bible or a book about God. Maybe they just had a conversation with you about faith and the questions that you were wrestling with. Maybe they held the door for you or went above and beyond for you in some way. Maybe they were a parent or grandparent, a youth pastor, a close friend. Whoever it may be, and whatever it is they did for you, they helped you get to where you are in your faith.

They were the Easter egg hiders, and the things they did for you to say yes to God were the Easter eggs.

What eggs are you hiding for the people in your own life?

You see, Jesus isn't supposed to be the best-kept secret. He's supposed to be our favorite topic of conversation.

This journey of following Him doesn't end once we find Him. Ever wonder why we stay on earth once we believe in God? If the only goal was to get to a place where we believe in Him, then why wouldn't we immediately be taken to Heaven? But instead, we're left here. The reason is that the script is supposed to flip, and we're supposed to take on the role of hiding Easter eggs for everyone else in our lives.

It would be wrong to end this book without sharing this truth. People die.

All the time, every day, every second—people die. Sometimes it's because of old age and after a full life, but sometimes it's not. What if your friend, coworker, family member, whoever had days left to live? Would you be helping to assure what their eternity will look like after they breathe their last?

"Woah, Mitch, this is a really dark way to end this section," you may be thinking.

Possibly. But it's also extremely real. And I personally am no stranger to people losing their lives way too young. I don't know about you, but not much haunts me more than the thought, "If I would've known that was the last time, what would I have said differently?"

If something has really gone missing, and this something is the thing that determines whether we spend forever in Heaven or Hell, we cannot keep it to ourselves.

I know the excuses that follow about not being good with words or not having a Bible degree or a position as a pastor or a church leader. Yeah, that's all great, but there is no excuse when you see what the Creator of the universe did for you. He gave up His own Son. You can give up a fraction of comfortability and even reputation for Him.

We need to be people who hide Easter eggs for others. Pray for others. Encourage others. Support others. Be there for others.

Love others. And be ready for when they look at you and say, "Okay what is different about you? How are you so peaceful? How are you so joyful? I want some of that!"

People notice when you live like Jesus, and when you do it the right way, they want in.

This is the most important thing you could give your life to. Tomorrow isn't promised. Therefore, it's time to get serious about what is missing and join the Easter egg hunting team.

Someone in your direct circle of influence needs you to show them who Jesus is. Are you missing out on that opportunity?

What if you were the only source of truth they had in their life? And instead of speaking out about your faith and what you believe, you kept it to yourself?

I'm not usually into this kind of stuff, but it feels right. I want you to stop reading this book for a moment. Grab your phone. Shoot a text to someone that doesn't know Jesus. If you can't think of anyone, it's time to expand who you interact with. But text that person (or a handful of people). Let them know that Jesus died for them. Maybe even invite them to go to church with you this week. If you're too nervous about what they'll think or what they'll say, you may not actually love them. Because this very truly is a matter of life and death. Something has gone missing, and this changes everything. Who are you keeping eternity from?

This should keep you up at night. Always being on guard and awake to those around you that God has placed in your life to use you as an instrument—an Easter egg hiding instrument.

Don't miss out on the never-ending discovery of showing the world who Jesus really is and what He's done for others.

This world needs it.

Needs you.

Desperately.

Get to hiding.

Two days.

It's been two days since the horrific day that your family experienced on Friday. At this point, your brother has been buried, and the three of you have begun to settle down at home and make sense of what is now the new normal for your household.

It's been quiet. Almost eerie at times.

Although your brother wasn't home all the time, his absence can be felt so much more now that he's gone for good.

"I assure you, today you will be with me in paradise."

Those words continue to repeat in your mind every time you think about that day. Which is a lot.

What did he mean by this? Could it be true? Was he really the Messiah? Does he have the power to say such a thing? What do I do with this memory burned into my mind? You ask yourself these questions over and over again, but you don't find much of an answer.

"I assure you, today you will be with me in paradise."

You can hear the exact tone of voice and candor that Jesus spoke with. You can picture the face of your brother as he broke into joyful tears upon hearing such a statement.

And then it hits you. *If that really was the Messiah, and He really did speak those words to my brother who didn't deserve to go to Heaven based on the way he lived his life, then what determines if a person is saved or not? People are going to say that this declaration to my brother was unfair based on the way he lived his life*, you think to yourself.

As you continue to run circles in your mind of what this could mean and try to explain this illogical move from the potential Son of God, there is a knock on your door.

"Yeah?" you ask, slightly annoyed that you're being interrupted.

Your parents walk in together, and an atmosphere of confusion immediately enters the room with them.

"What's going on?" you ask.

"Do you know that man that was next to your brother on Friday? The one who was in the middle?" your father asks you.

Oh don't I remember him, you think to yourself, but you respond out loud, "Um yeah, the one who was claiming to be the King of the Jews."

"Yeah him—well, there's been some news about him. If you come outside, you'll hear the streets full of people talking about it and trying to figure it out," your dad continues.

"News? He's dead? Was it his followers that tore the veil in the Temple or something?" you ask, eagerly waiting for his response.

"No, it's a little bit more than that," your dad chuckles slightly and then continues on, "He um—He's back. Back from the dead."

You immediately jump up from where you were sitting, unsure of what to say or do next, but you can feel that your jaw is essentially on the floor at this point.

"So, does this mean that He is actually who He said He is? He is the Son of God?" you exclaim.

"Well, I never thought I'd say this, but if you look at the prophecies and things conveyed about the Messiah in the Old Testament, how could He not be?" your dad says.

You run by them and out into the street, and you see the people buzzing and talking about this thing that has happened. You hear claims about the holes being in His hands and the scars on His sides. You hear the rumors that the stone in front of His tomb was moved, and it was completely empty inside. There are people singing and dancing and rejoicing over the fact that this man is back from the dead.

Standing there, right in front of your house, seeing the atmosphere of the town and hearing the things being said, you are brought to tears. You can't believe that this has happened, and your brother, who had been running from God almost his entire life, whose reputation had been stained and hopeless to the people around you, had been redeemed by the Son of God Himself.

As you continue to cry, you fall to your knees as your heart is moved to belief. For the first time in your life, you find yourself moved by who God is. Then, because of everything that you've seen and heard in those last couple days, you begin to believe like you never have before.

Your parents open the front door to find you in this position, and after pulling yourself together a little bit, you explain to them everything that you've been thinking and feeling, and they admit that conversations had been very similar between them.

Your brother believed and was saved only moments before he died. There were no exceptions. No course correction. No standard that he didn't meet. No catch. Just belief in who Jesus said that He was.

You can't believe that this amazing moment is now a part of your story. You can't believe you've witnessed what you've witnessed. You can't believe that history has been changed, and the long-awaited Messiah died, hanging next to your brother.

You can't wait to go and tell others about this.

Some will say it's unfair. Some will say it doesn't add up. Some will say that he's not in Heaven due to the things that he's done.

And they might be right. It wasn't fair. It doesn't add up. But that's all the more reason to tell others about the amazing grace of God that you've witnessed.

People need to know that belief in God and what His Son has done on the cross can change everything. Not being good enough. Not the right words. But believing in your heart.

Thanks to your brother's act of faith, you were a witness to this. Now you have no option but to go tell the world about the life-altering love of Jesus.

☦

I feel like it's fitting to start and end this chapter with the topic of Easter.

As I said, I've always loved Easter. Growing up, I loved the

Easter egg hunts, dressing up for church on that Sunday, all of the good candy, and being around family. But the older that I get, I love it even more because I understand that without the story of Easter, one of the most important pieces to the puzzle that is Jesus wouldn't be there. If His story ended with the crucifixion (Good Friday as it's called), then a lot of history and people alive at that time would stick with Him just being a good teacher or a guy out of his mind or a martyr of the faith.

But the story didn't end on that Friday. The final word wasn't His death.

Sunday was coming.

From our point of view in history, it came! And with it came the victory over death, Hell, and even the grave. That same victory is available to you and me. You see, when the cost of our sin goes missing, and we believe in Jesus and accept this gift of freedom, we are covered by His blood. When we die, this becomes our only ticket to Heaven.

The Bible tells us, time and time again, that we deserved Hell. You and I both deserved to spend eternity after we die separated from God forever. But the story has been rewritten. Jesus changed the ending by dying on the cross for us and then rising from the dead as a symbol of His power and His authority over death.

That's pretty cool if you ask me.

We serve a God who has authority and victory over death—something that 100 percent of us reading this are going to face. We serve a God who says, "It is finished."

Not even death—something that will meet each and every person no matter how good or put together or successful they are—could stop Jesus. He stared it in the face, took it head on, and beat it.

Jesus did it for you and for me so that we no longer have to fear death or separation from God. Instead, we can know that Jesus won our victory for us, and if we believe in Him, that victory becomes ours, too.

Anyone else feeling pumped up?

This gets me so excited. Like I could run through a brick wall.

The heart behind this book has been to get you to see that something has gone missing, and what has gone missing is a really good thing. It's potentially the best thing.

The goal has been to show you the beautiful God of the Bible and how He is holy, perfect, and so powerful. Yet He made an unfair decision from our human point of view that was in our favor by sending His Son to earth to die in our place. Without that sacrifice, we are broken and hopeless by definition of being a human. But through Jesus' sacrifice, we are set free, and the debt that we were in because of our sin (doesn't matter what the specific sin was or is) has gone missing. We just have to accept that gift of Jesus on the cross. We can stand before God and follow God wholeheartedly and confidently—not because of anything we've done but because of what's been done for us. The heart behind this book was to paint that picture and challenge you to share it with the world around you.

That's what this has all been about.

But there's something else.

Something else has gone missing that has allowed for us to have even more confidence and joy while we follow God. Something else has gone missing that has taken away any doubts and fears that we may have and replaced them with passion and love for our God. "What else has gone missing?" you wonder.

Jesus is missing from the grave.

That, my friends, is why we can stare down any trial, persecution, addiction, struggle, opposition, stronghold, or the devil himself and know that they've already been defeated. They've already been made fools out of because our God has won the victory and defeated the sting of death and the power of Hell.

Not only this but when we believe in Him, and something goes missing in our lives when we become covered by the blood of Jesus, that victory becomes a shared one. We get to experience and walk in the freedom and celebration that Jesus earned on the cross and in the grave.

Cue the fireworks and Disney World trips.

Jesus' victory has become ours. Our God isn't selfish with it, but He gives away this victory when we believe in Him and follow Him with our lives.

Something is missing. It's the weight of your sin. And it's time to replace the gap that is left behind with undistracted love and dedication to Jesus.

I mean, after all, He is the only One who deserves it.

TREASURE #3 -
WHEN WE UNDERSTAND THE IMPORTANCE OF JESUS ALLOWING THE COST OF OUR SIN TO GO MISSING AND HE HIMSELF GOING MISSING FROM THE GRAVE, WE ARE RELEASED INTO THE REST OF THE WORLD WITH A PASSION AND DESIRE TO SEE OTHERS COME TO KNOW HIM AS WELL. WHEN WE REALLY UNDERSTAND WHAT JESUS HAS DONE FOR US, THERE ISN'T ANY OTHER OPTION BUT TO TELL OTHER PEOPLE ABOUT IT. WE LOVE TO TALK ABOUT OUR HOBBIES AND THINGS WE'RE PASSIONATE ABOUT. HOPEFULLY, THIS BOOK HAS PUSHED US TO SEE THAT JESUS BELONGS ON THAT LIST.

X MARKS THE SPOT

Wow. You did it. You finished this book. Or maybe you just skipped to this section. If so... you're a cheater. I wanted to end a book like this that is with a quick summary of the path we've walked and the things we've learned. The reason why is because if this book is just a book, I've missed the point. If this book just goes on some shelf or in a drawer and nothing comes out of your life because of it then these past two years of my life have been a waste. I want this book to serve as a guide and a toolkit to help us better discover what has gone missing, and help others find it as well.

THE PROBLEM

CLUE #1 - THE FACT THAT SOMETHING IS MISSING MAY BE FOR OUR GOOD.

CLUE #2 - IF YOUR GOAL IS TO MEASURE UP, YOU'RE GOING TO FALL SHORT EVERY SINGLE TIME (SO CHANGE YOUR GOAL).

CLUE #3 - A PERFECT GOD CANNOT EXIST WITH SIN. BUT THAT'S WHO WE ARE. HOW CAN WE REACH THE LEVEL OF GOD'S APPROVAL? WE NEED SOMETHING TO BE ADDED TO THE EQUATION. OR SOMETHING TO GO MISSING FROM THE RECORD.

CLUE #4 - EVERYONE HAS FALLEN SHORT OF GOD'S DESIRE, AND WE CANNOT MAKE THINGS RIGHT ON OUR OWN BECAUSE OUR SIN, MISTAKES, GUILT, AND SHAME STAND IN THE WAY. WE'RE ALL MURDERERS. IF NOT IN ACTIONS, WE DEFINITELY ARE IN OUR HEARTS AND MINDS. BUT JESUS HAS TAKEN SOMETHING AWAY, ERASED IT COMPLETELY, AND THIS CHANGES OUR ETERNAL DESTINY.

THE PATH

KEY #1 - GOD'S HEART HAS NEVER BEEN TO OPPRESS OR CONTROL YOU. HE'S GOD. ALL-POWERFUL. ALMIGHTY. IF HE WANTED TO CONTROL YOU, HE COULD. BUT HIS HEART FOR YOU AND FOR HUMANITY SINCE THE BEGINNING OF TIME HAS BEEN TO WALK ALONGSIDE US, LOVE US UNCONDITIONALLY, AND SHOW US THAT HIS WAYS ARE ACTUALLY THE KEY FOR US TO FIND TRUE JOY, PEACE, AND HAPPINESS.

KEY #2 - THE ONLY WAY TO EXPERIENCE ETERNAL LIFE IN HEAVEN AND FULL LIFE ON EARTH IS THROUGH JESUS AND WHAT HE DID ON THE CROSS. WE ARE NOT POWERFUL ENOUGH TO EARN OUR WAY TO HEAVEN OR QUALIFIED ON OUR OWN, BUT BECAUSE OF WHAT'S MISSING, WE HAVE BEEN MADE ENOUGH THROUGH THE ONE WHO HAS ALWAYS BEEN MORE THAN ENOUGH

KEY #3 - THE EVIDENCE IN YOUR CASE IS STACKED AGAINST YOU, BUT IT HAS GONE MISSING. AND IF IT WERE THERE, YOU'D BE CONVICTED TO A LIFE SENTENCE OF SEPARATION AND SUFFERING. BUT IF YOU BELIEVE IN JESUS AND WHAT HE'S DONE, THE SCALE IS BROKEN IN YOUR FAVOR. THIS IS WHERE FREEDOM IS FOUND.

KEY #4 - YOUR IDENTITY HAS BEEN REDEEMED. YOU'RE NO LONGER JUST A NUMBER IN THE WORLD, BUT YOU'RE

KNOWN, LOVED, CALLED, CHOSEN, PROTECTED, AND CONNECTED TO THE CREATOR OF THE UNIVERSE. NOT ONLY THAT, BUT THIS IDENTITY HAS BEEN EARNED AND GIVEN TO YOU BY JESUS! IT CANNOT BE TAKEN AWAY BY OUR MISTAKES. THIS FACT SHOULD MATTER MORE THAN ANYTHING ELSE! CHOOSE TO LIVE THAT WAY!

THE PROPOSITION

TREASURE #1 - WHEN WE LOVE GOD MORE THAN OURSELVES, WE WILL QUICKLY FIND TRUE JOY, PEACE, AND LIFE. WE NEED TO STOP MAKING EXCUSES, STOP BEING SELF-CENTERED, AND START DISCOVERING IN GOD'S WORD WHAT HE CALLS US TO DO. AND WHEN ALL ELSE FAILS, WE NEED TO FILL OUR LIVES WITH MORE THANKFULNESS AND WORSHIP BECAUSE OUR GOD HAD EVERY RIGHT TO CANCEL US BUT DIDN'T! WE ARE STUCK IN HIS LOVE! LET IT CHANGE US FROM THE INSIDE OUT.

TREASURE #2 - WE CAN HAVE CONFIDENCE AND ASSURANCE IN WHO WE ARE BECAUSE OF WHO GOD IS AND WHAT HE SAYS ABOUT US. WE NO LONGER HAVE TO SEEK OR CHASE AFTER GOD'S APPROVAL BECAUSE WE UNDERSTAND FULL WELL THAT GOD APPROVES THOSE WHO HAVE BEEN SET FREE BY THE BLOOD OF JESUS. IF WE BECOME ROOTED IN THE IDENTITY JESUS HAS EARNED FOR US, IT CHANGES THE WAY WE TALK, THINK, TREAT OTHERS, AND LIVE OUR LIVES EVERY SINGLE DAY.

TREASURE #3 - WHEN WE UNDERSTAND THE IMPORTANCE OF JESUS ALLOWING THE COST OF OUR SIN TO GO MISSING AND HE HIMSELF GOING MISSING FROM THE GRAVE, WE ARE RELEASED INTO THE REST OF THE WORLD WITH A PASSION AND DESIRE TO SEE OTHERS COME TO KNOW HIM AS WELL. WHEN WE REALLY UNDERSTAND

WHAT JESUS HAS DONE FOR US, THERE ISN'T ANY OTHER OPTION BUT TO TELL OTHER PEOPLE ABOUT IT. WE LOVE TO TALK ABOUT OUR HOBBIES AND THINGS WE'RE PASSIONATE ABOUT. HOPEFULLY, THIS BOOK HAS PUSHED US TO SEE THAT JESUS BELONGS ON THAT LIST.

ABOUT THE AUTHOR

Mitch Frost is a student pastor, communicator, and author based out of Columbus, Ohio whose heartbeat is for the next generation to experience the life changing love of Jesus.

Mitch and his wife, Lexi, spend their time doing ministry together and share the desire to see the world shaped by God's Word. Their first daughter, Charlotte, made them a family of three in early 2023.

Head on over to www.mitchfrost.org to connect with him and find out what else is going on in their world!

CPSIA information can be obtained
at www.ICGtesting.com
Printed in the USA
JSHW020846210523
41985JS00001B/64

9 781664 292048